Policing Matters

Policing and Young People

Policing Matters

Policing and Young People

Edited by Tim Read
and
Colin Rogers

Series editors: P A J Waddington
and
Martin Wright

LearningMatters

First published in 2011 by Learning Matters Ltd

British Library Cataloguing in Publication Data
A CIP record for this book is available from the British Library.

ISBN: 978 0 85725 477 1

This book is also available in the following ebook formats:

Adobe ebook   ISBN: 978 0 85725 479 5
EPUB ebook   ISBN: 978 0 85725 478 8
Kindle   ISBN: 978 0 85725 480 1

Cover and text design by Toucan Design
Project Management by Newgen Publishing and Data Services
Typeset by Newgen Publishing and Data Services
Printed and bound in Great Britain by Short Run Press Ltd, Exeter, Devon

Learning Matters Ltd
20 Cathedral Yard
Exeter EX1 1HB
Tel: 01392 215560
info@learningmatters.co.uk
www.learningmatters.co.uk

All weblinks and web addresses in this book have been carefully checked prior to publication, but for up-to-date information please visit the Learning Matters website, www.learningmatters.co.uk.

Contents

1 Introduction: policing and young people

Introduction

The relationship between the police and young people is important. Young people experience crime, as perpetrators and victims, more than any other sector of the population, with the most persistent offenders often those most at risk of victimisation. However, despite the importance of this relationship, government and policing policy has tended to focus on young people as offenders and, perhaps as a reflection of this, young people are now less likely to have confidence in the police than other age groups.

(Oxford Policing Policy Forum, 2010, p 1)

This book is about the relationship between the police and young people. Over the past 15 years or so, many of the developments that have taken place around policing, and the roles that the police have had to assume, have been inextricably linked to young people: young people as offenders, young people as victims (across a variety of offence types and in a variety of circumstances), young people as witnesses of crime and young people as the focus of anti-social behaviour and disorder. This book aims to provide an overview of the contact that occurs between the police and young people and to explore and explain the nature of this contact.

In the 'rationale for intervention' produced in July 2008 by the relevant government departments (Home Office, Department for Children, Schools and Families and the Ministry of Justice, 2008), and building on the same year's 'Youth Crime Action Plan', it was suggested that the *economic rationale for intervening to tackle youth offending and reoffending is based on the argument that youth crime is a 'public bad' because the harm it causes extends beyond the individuals committing it. There is a high cost to society not only in terms of the consequences of crime (e.g. value of property stolen, property damaged, victim services, lost output, physical and emotional impact) and the costs of responding to it (e.g. cost of the criminal justice system) but also in terms of the costs associated with anticipation of crime (e.g. costs of insurance and security measures)* (Home Office, Department for Children, Schools and Families and the Ministry of Justice, 2008, p 3).

To support this claim, the document stated that in 1996 the National Audit Office estimated that the annual funding of services directly involved with young offenders cost around £1 billion. In addition, the report asserted that there was a *high long-term cost to young people committing crime because we know that crime is associated with a range of poor economic and social outcomes. Preventing youth crime can therefore reduce these economic and social costs* (Home Office, Department for Children, Schools and Families and the Ministry of Justice, 2008, p 3).

The current government's recent consultation document on criminal justice (Breaking the Cycle: Effective Punishment, Rehabilitation and Sentencing of Offenders) states in its foreword that it is *not acceptable that 75 per cent of offenders sentenced to youth custody reoffend within a year. If we do not prevent and tackle offending by young people then the young offenders of today will become the prolific career criminals of tomorrow* (Ministry of Justice, 2010, p 1). Attempts to prevent youth offending remain high on the list of the government's priorities, and the police play a central role in this.

The government has also undertaken a review into the way that anti-social behaviour is dealt with by the police, examining the sanctions available to them and other agencies, in the light of research by Her Majesty's Inspectorate of Constabulary (2010) that was highly critical of the quality of service provided to members of the public (Home Office, 2011). Again, in the terms of this review, much attention has been focused upon the behaviour of young people, the extent to which their behaviour can be defined as anti-social and the way that they are policed.

Overview

The next three chapters of this book look at the nature of the relationship between the police and young people and attempt to explain why the two groups come into such frequent contact.

Chapter 2 examines the experience of young people as victims of crime and as offenders. It looks at the nature of offending by young people and identifies a number of risk factors associated with this offending. It also examines the experience of young people as victims of crime, looking at the extent of repeat victimisation among the young and the types of offences they are victims of.

In Chapter 3, Colin Rogers looks at issues around perceptions: perceptions about young people held by the public and the police and young peoples' perception of the police. He examines the extent to which the behaviour of young people has always been depicted as problematic (notably through the notion of 'moral panic'). In particular, the chapter looks at the role of the media in determining the way that young people are depicted and the extent to which this has coloured the way that the police interact with young people.

This theme is continued in Chapter 4 (Anti-Social Behaviour and Young People) which looks at the increased focus there has been on anti-social behaviour over the past 15 years and the extent to which anti-social behaviour has become a shorthand for the public behaviour of young people – largely because of their public visibility. The chapter also examines what this has meant in terms of relations between the police and young people, and the development and use of sanctions (particularly the Anti-Social Behaviour Order) to tackle anti-social behaviour.

Chapter 5 looks at the structures in the criminal justice system that have been developed specifically to cater for young people: youth courts, the youth justice board and youth offending teams (YOTs). The chapter looks in detail at the work of YOTs and at the attempts that have been made to divert young offenders (or those deemed to be at risk of offending) away from the criminal justice system, including the role that reparation and restorative justice have played in recent youth justice policy.

Chapter 6 develops a number of the themes considered in Chapter 5, in particular, efforts to divert young people away from the formal criminal justice system. It considers the nature of police engagement with young people and the role of police discretion. It discusses different models of crime prevention and the role of social crime prevention in trying to build crime-resistant communities. The role of youth engagement is examined in this context, particularly the development of Youth Inclusion Programmes and Safer School Partnerships.

The remaining chapters of the book look in detail at some specific areas of work that the police are likely to undertake with young people. In Chapter 7, Harriet Pierpoint considers the factors that have to be borne in mind by police officers when dealing with young people as suspects. Following a consideration of the conditions that apply to juvenile detention in police stations, she examines the role of responsible adults in relation to young people: the history of the role, who can act as an appropriate adult and what research indicates about the effectiveness of those who act in the role (parents, volunteers and social workers).

In Chapter 8, Patrick Tucker considers the legal and developmental issues that affect children as witnesses. These issues affect how young people's evidence is obtained and received within the Criminal Justice System, within the child safeguarding arena, and its associated procedures. Identifying how important landmark cases and reviews have influenced the development of law and practice relating to young people as witnesses, the chapter provides an overview of the basic issues of reliability, credibility and compellability of child witnesses and links these issues to the legislation and investigative guidance that is utilised by professional practitioners who deal with young people as witnesses.

Finally, in Chapter 9, the issues involved in safeguarding young people (what used to be termed 'child protection') are considered by Patrick Tucker and Gerwyn Henderson. This chapter looks at the way that safeguarding policy and practice has emerged, often in response to failings by the police and medical and social services in cases with a high media profile.

By the end of the book you should have a clearer perspective on why the police find themselves dealing with young people on a frequent basis, the varied nature of the contact between the police and the young people and the specific operational and legislative requirements that relate to this contact.

Structure of the book

The book is organised around a series of reflective and practical tasks. These are designed to give you the opportunity to relate the material that has been provided in the chapter to your personal experience and to examine the extent to which you have understood the material in the book. Case studies illustrate issues explored by offering real-life examples. In addition, at the end of each chapter, further reading and useful websites are identified with the aim of allowing you to develop your knowledge of the area in more depth should you wish to do so.

REFERENCES

Her Majesty's Inspectorate of Constabulary (2010) *Anti-Social Behaviour; Stop the Rot.* London: HMIC.

Home Office, Department for Children, Schools and Families and Ministry of Justice (2008) *Impact Assessment of the Youth Crime Action Plan.* Available online at www.ialibrary.berr. gov.uk/uploaded/IA%20youth-crime-impact-assessment.pdf (accessed 23 March 2011).

Home Office (2011) *More Effective Responses to Anti-Social Behaviour.* London: Home Office. Available online at www.homeoffice.gov.uk/publications/consultations/cons-2010-antisocial-behaviour/asb-consultation-document?view=Binary (accessed 9 February 2011).

Ministry of Justice (2010) *Breaking the Cycle: Effective Punishment, Rehabilitation and Sentencing of Offenders.* London: Ministry of Justice.

Oxford Policing Policy Forum (2010) *Are Young People Over-Policed and Under-Protected?* Report of the 9th Oxford Policing Policy Forum, December 2010. Available online at www. police-foundation.org.uk/files/POLICE0001/oxfordforum/9th%20OPPF%20report.pdf (accessed 15 March 2011).

2 Young people as offenders and victims

CHAPTER OBJECTIVES

By the end of this chapter you should have a clearer understanding of:

- historical definitions of crime and young people;
- young people as offenders and victims of crime;
- the nature of youth offending;
- risk factors and predictors of offending by, and victimisation of, young people.

LINKS TO STANDARDS

The material in this chapter links to the Skills for Justice, National Occupational Standards Policing and Law Enforcement (2010).

HA1	(MLA1) Manage your own resources.
HA2	(MLA2) Manage your own resources and professional development.
POL 4C1	Develop one's own knowledge and practice.
SFJ AE1	Maintain and develop your own knowledge, skills and competence.

Introduction

This chapter considers patterns of crime and young people both as offenders and as victims. It includes a historical perspective, considering perceived changes over time, and a discussion of possible explanations for the patterns found. In particular, attention is given to important factors that appear to influence young offenders and victims and the extent to which these also change over time. The chapter further discusses risk factors considered to influence young people to become offenders and factors that may influence young victims of crime.

Young people and crime

Defining young people

The legal definition of a young person is not as straightforward as you might think. For example, the Children Act 1989 (Home Office, 1989) defines a 'child' as a person under the age of 18, while the Management of Health and Safety Regulations 1999 (Home Office, 1999) regard a 'child' as a person who is not over the minimum school-leaving age and a 'young person' as a person who has not attained the age of 18.

REFLECTIVE TASK

Look at the definition of 'youth' provided on the United Nations website at www. un.org/esa/socdev/unyin/qanda.htm.

Contrast this with the definitions provided in the 1933 Children and Young Person's Act (section 46, available at www.opsi.gov.uk/RevisedStatutes/Acts/ukpga/1933/ cukpga_19330012_en_5#pt3-pb1-l1g32), the Criminal Justice Act 1988 (Part III section 33 'Evidence of Persons under 14 in Committal Proceedings' available at www.opsi.gov.uk/acts/acts1988/ukpga_19880033_en_5#pt3-l1g33), the 1991 Criminal Justice Act (schedule 8 'Amendments for Treating Persons Aged 17 as Young Persons' available at www.opsi.gov.uk/acts/acts1991/ukpga_19910053_ en_16#sch8) and the Gillick Case (found at www.hrcr.org/safrica/childrens_rights/ Gillick_WestNorfolk.htm).

Why do you think these definitions differ, and why have they evolved?

Young people and crime in context

The notion of childhood and children as we understand them is a fairly recent concept. In the past, paintings tended to show children as angelic forms, perhaps as a reminder of the very high mortality rate prevalent until recent times. Up until the Middle Ages, children were depicted as little adults and regarded as such in society, being granted no special favours for their age (Aries, 1996). In Victorian times, many children were still regarded as small adults and were expected to work and be treated as such by the law, police and the whole of the criminal justice system (Chesney, 1991). Understanding what Brown (1998) refers to as the pre-history of youth and crime is important as it helps us understand that we have existing perceptions based upon different states of human development. For many people, middle age is aligned to respectability, while old age stands for vulnerability. Similarly, for many, the concept of youth is viewed as being problematic and something to be feared. In more recent times, however, the identification and targeting of children and young persons for proactive policing has been typically justified in the name of child welfare, crime prevention and public protection (Muncie, 2009).

Historical perspective

The presence of young people has always attracted the concern and attention of adults. Pearson (1983) highlights the concerns in a report on the question of juvenile crime and misbehaviour published in 1898. The words in the report may almost have been written today.

> *The general impression running through its pages was a riot of impunity, irresponsible parents, working mothers, and lax discipline in schools, with magistrates and police believing themselves to be impotent before a rising tide of mischief and violence.*
>
> (Pearson, 1983, p 55)

Long before this report was published, however, young people and their involvement in criminal activity drew attention. In 1585, it is reported that in London, a man called Wooton, once a merchant but falling on hard times, took to running a school for thieves. Young boys learned to cut purses from passers-by in the streets, and merchants complained of gangs of young people entering their premises, and while being distracted by one or two of them, the remainder would steal articles (Salgado, 1999).

Throughout history, therefore, some young people have been associated with forms of undesirable activity: think about the 'Teddy Boy' craze in the United Kingdom in the 1950s (Pearson, 1983) and the Mods and Rockers of the 1960s (Cohen, 1973). A historical line can be traced which links many activities undertaken by young people and which appears to cause consternation among society. Nothing is new. For example, a recent activity known as 'Happy Slapping' was reported by the media as being of major concern.

CASE STUDY: HAPPY SLAPPING

The BBC news website on the 12 May 2005 reported that 'a new trend of violent assaults, in which teenagers attack unsuspecting bystanders and capture it on mobile phones, has spread to Kent. "Happy slapping" first began as a craze in south London, but has now become a nationwide phenomenon, according to police and anti-bullying organisations. Footage passed to the BBC showed an assault at a Ramsgate skateboard park. A school in Tonbridge has also warned that a boy's hearing has been damaged' (http://news.bbc.co.uk/1/hi/england/4539317.stm).

Clearly, the idea of 'youth annoyance' and illegal activities committed by young people is not a new one, and the idea that there is a decline in the standards of behaviour of young people needs to be viewed in this light.

Young people, culture and locations

Police and young people predominantly seem to interact in public locations such as the street, and invariably this involves disputes over ownership of 'turf', language used, etc. Typically, this involves the street-corner scenario or outside shops, city centres and other high-profile locations. Many of these locations have significance for young people, which can promote a sense of territory and an area for their own brand of entertainment (Webster, 2006). In such circumstances, interactions between police and young people appear to be highly racialised and gendered. In the United Kingdom, black young people appear especially vulnerable to 'proactive' policing, being up to six times as likely to be stopped and searched as white youths. When black young people come into contact with the police, whether as victims or witnesses, their perceptions and experiences of police tend to be worse than for white young people.

Further, Loader (1996) suggests that from interviews conducted with police officers, one of the most common and consistent views is that young people hanging about in groups will be either directly or indirectly involved in criminal behaviour. This view tends to affect the perceptions of the general public as well, irrespective of what the evidence suggests.

Public perceptions of young people and crime

Much of what we know statistically regarding young people as offenders and as victims comes from official documents such as that produced by the National Association for the Care and Rehabilitation of Offenders (NACRO, 2009) which in turn is based upon official crime statistics (Ministry of Justice, 2007), and the British Crime Survey (available at www.homeoffice.gov.uk/rds/bcs1.html).

Despite falling levels of victimisation, most members of the public at a national level continue to believe that crime is rising. During 2007–08, almost two-thirds of those surveyed considered that crime had risen in the past two years, while 35 per cent thought that it had increased 'a lot' (a two per cent rise over the previous 12 months). Despite the perception that crime is rising, fear of crime – for a range of offence types – is steadily falling. For instance, the proportion of people expressing high levels of worry about violent crime has declined from 25 per cent in 1998 to 15 per cent in 2007–08. Over the same period, concern about burglary has also fallen from 19 per cent to 12 per cent of those surveyed (NACRO, 2009).

Concern about crime is highest among:

• those who have been a victim within the past 12 months;

• residents of areas classified as 'hard pressed';

• black and minority ethnic respondents;

• women.

Those surveyed considered that the main causes of offending were drugs (30 per cent) and lack of discipline from parents (29 per cent), both of which might be thought to indicate that offending by younger people is a particular focus of disquiet. The third most frequently cited causal factor was sentencing being too lenient (11 per cent) (NACRO, 2009).

At the same time, public confidence in the ability of the criminal justice system to deal with young people accused of crime is considerably lower than any other function about which questions were posed: while 80 per cent of those surveyed considered that the criminal justice system respected the rights of people accused of crime, just one in four thought that it was able to deal effectively with young people who offend.

Young people as offenders

The characteristics of young people who offend

Research conducted on young people who come into contact with the youth justice system has found that they are statistically more likely to share certain characteristics than those who do not.

PRACTICAL TASK

Think about the risk factors that may be prevalent for young people and that may influence their involvement with the criminal justice system as offenders. Write down what you think they are.

These 'risk factors' are typically presented as clustering around four domains.

1. Family – including inadequate, harsh or inconsistent parenting.

2. School/education – such as low educational attainment, truancy or exclusion.

3. Community – including residence in areas with low community cohesion and easy access to drugs.

4. Individual/personal – such as being male, having an offending peer group, poor physical or mental health or misuse of alcohol or drugs.

Such risk factors are generally familiar to those who work within the youth justice system. They are at the heart of the assessment model used by Youth Offending Teams (visit www.yjb.gov.uk/en-gb/yjs/YouthOffendingTeams/ for more about Youth Offending Teams). They also constitute the basis for the development of the Youth Justice Board's *'scaled approach'* which seeks to link the intensity of intervention to the risk of reoffending, indicated by the score derived from *Asset*, the Board's assessment tool. While this approach is useful, it must be remembered that many individuals identified as 'high risk' do not offend. Similarly, many children identified as 'low risk' do offend, and inevitably, the picture is rather more complex than frequently suggested.

It is sometimes suggested that a focus on the four domains, described above, as separate clusters of risk of equal weight tends to underestimate the impact of the area in which young people grow up. Pitts (2007) in his study of gangs has argued persuasively that involvement in certain sorts of serious crime may be more closely associated with residence in disadvantaged neighbourhoods than with the individual, familial or educational characteristics of the children who live there. Indeed, to a large extent, concentrations of poverty within communities are themselves likely to have a negative impact on parenting capacity within resident families and on the educational achievement of children in the area, and may increase the risk that young people will come into contact with drugs or groups of offending peers.

Victimisation and young people

Finally, one individual risk factor merits further attention. It is well established that teenagers have a significantly higher risk of victimisation than adults. Moreover, within the younger age group, the chances of being a victim are not evenly distributed. Rather the characteristics of those most likely to be victimised mirror closely the risk factors for offending. One study (Stewart et al., 2002) has suggested that, in relation to violent crime at least, the pathways from victimisation to offending – and vice versa – are so closely intertwined that frequently it makes little sense to talk in categorical terms about victims or offenders but rather winners or losers in any given incident. Certainly, in 2006, half of 10- to 15-year-olds who admitted offending had experienced criminal victimisation within the previous 12 months compared to just 19 per cent of those who had committed no offence. Conversely, victims were more likely to admit offending (42 per cent) than those who had no experience of victimisation within the previous 12 months (14 per cent) (NACRO, 2009).

Whatever model is used to identify children and young people who may be at risk of offending, it is clear that the majority of those who come to the attention of the youth justice system are typically socially excluded, come from the most disadvantaged sections of the community and have the fewest opportunities open to them.

Detected youth crime

As discussed previously, public perception is not necessarily a good indicator of trends in crime. In addition, discovering the extent of youth crime is not as straightforward as it would seem. There are a number of reasons for this. Firstly, only a minor percentage of those children who admit committing offences come into contact with the youth justice system. During 2006, for instance, 30 per cent of young people aged 10–17 years admitted having committed an offence within the past 12 months, but just 5 per cent were arrested. In part, this difference can be explained by the fact that most crimes are not reported to the police anyway. During 2007–08, for instance, well under half of all offences (42 per cent) were brought to police attention. Three-quarters of victims who did not report an offence indicated that this was because the incident was too trivial, the loss involved was minimal or there was little that the police could do.

In the case of violent crime, 35 per cent of respondents considered that it was a private matter that they would deal with themselves. It seems likely, therefore, that a significant proportion of self-reported offending by young people, similar to all other types of offenders, is at a level of seriousness such that the victims do not pursue the matter formally through the criminal justice system. Where crimes are reported, detection rates remain low. During 2007–08, the proportion of offences recorded by the police that were 'cleared up' was 28 per cent, and where the perpetrator was not caught (as is the case for almost three-quarters of crime reported to the police), it was not possible to attribute responsibility for an offence or determine whether it was committed by a young person or an adult. The figures for detected crime, thus, only tell part of the story but they do, nonetheless, suggest that young people are more likely than adults to offend (NACRO, 2009).

Age and detections

During 2007, the peak age of offending was 17 years for males and 15 years for females, and there were 6,433 and 2,203 indictable offences per 100,000 of the population in those two age groups, respectively; the comparable rate for all ages was 1,082 offences per 100,000. At the same time, adults account for the major part of the total volume of crime simply because there are more people over the age of 18 years. So during 2007, children and young people committed fewer than one in five of all detected offences. Adults aged 21 years and above, by contrast, were responsible for more than two-thirds of offences. The bar chart in Figure 2.1 illustrates the differences in detections by age.

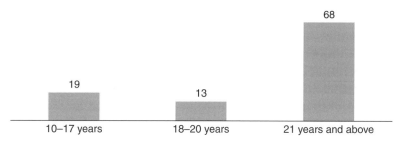

Figure 2.1 Percentage of detected offending by age
Source: NACRO (2009)

Trends in youth crime

From the early 1990s until 2003, *Criminal Statistics* (Ministry of Justice, 2007) showed a substantial decline in detected youth crime. Over that period, despite public concerns that youth crime was rising, the volume of youth offending fell by 27 per cent. However, more recently, there has been a reversal of that trend, as shown in the chart in Figure 2.2 below. During 2007, 126,000 children and young people aged 10–17 received a reprimand, final warning or conviction for an indictable offence, and this, while still some 12 per cent lower than the equivalent figure for 1992, represents an increase of 20 per cent since 2003.

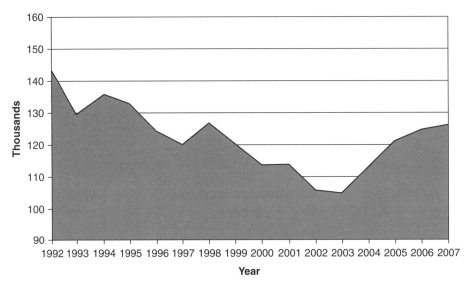

Figure 2.2 Children and young people cautioned, reprimanded, warned or sentenced for indictable offences, 1992–2007

Source: NACRO (2009)

The above shifts are not fully explicable in terms of fluctuations in the youth population. The fall and subsequent rise in youth crime appear as sharp even when demographic change is taken into account. So the proportion of 15- to 17-year-old males receiving a substantive disposal for an indictable offence was 7,065 for every 100,000 of the population in that age group in 1992 compared with 5,360 in 2003. As the *volume* of detected offences has risen for this age group in the more recent period, so too has the *rate* of offending: to 5,959 per 100,000 of the population in 2007.

Until 2003, the pattern of detected crime committed by young adults, aged 18–20 years, followed a trajectory similar to that for children and young people. The recent departure for the latter group from the trend dominant in that earlier period has not been accompanied by an equivalent increase in detected offending by young adults, or persons over the age of 21 years, which has remained comparatively stable.

Cessation of offending

Read McNeill's (2002) publication 'Beyond 'What Works': How and Why Do People Stop Offending?' (available at www.cjsw.ac.uk/cjsw/files/Briefing%20Paper%205_ final.pdf).

Consider and evaluate the various explanations that are given as to why people cease to offend, and why the impact of these factors might change over time.

Age and offenders

Between 1988 and 2002, the peak age of detected offending for boys was consistently 18 years. In 2002, it rose to 19 before falling to 18 again in 2003. It has been 17 in each of the four subsequent years for which data are available. The peak age for detected female offending was 15 years in 2007, as it has been for a considerable number of years. As a consequence, two-thirds of young people coming into contact with the youth justice system fall within the 15- to 17-year age bracket, 31 per cent between 12 and 14 years and just 3 per cent below the age of 12 (NACRO, 2009).

There has nonetheless been a significant age-related shift since 2003. While the number of young people aged 15–17 years who received a reprimand, final warning or conviction for an indictable offence grew by 20 per cent between 2003 and 2007, the equivalent increase for younger children aged 10–14 years was 31 per cent. As the chart in Figure 2.3 below illustrates, the overall rise in detected

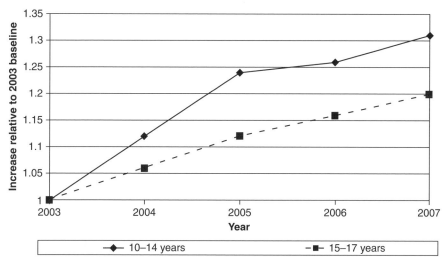

Figure 2.3 Relative increases in detected crime by age, 2003–07

Source: NACRO (2009)

crime in the recent period involves a disproportionate criminalisation of children below the age of 15 years.

This pattern is most readily explained as a consequence of changes in police decision-making pursuant to the sanction detection targets which will be discussed at some length in the chapter dedicated to anti-social behaviour. It is consistent with the use of formal responses to children's behaviour that would previously have been dealt with outside of the youth justice system since one would expect any such change to be reflected most sharply among younger children who would previously have been most likely to benefit from informal action.

Gender

Girls are consistently less likely than their male counterparts to come into contact with the youth justice system. During 2007, almost three-quarters (74 per cent) of young people convicted, warned or reprimanded for an indictable offence were male. Girls also tend to stop offending at an earlier age, and desistance is more rapid than among boys.

There is a common perception that the involvement of girls in offending has been rising for some years. Despite increases in detected female crime since 2003, the official statistics over the earlier period do not support a sustained trend in that direction over the longer term; indeed, between 1992 and 2002, the number of girls receiving a caution, reprimand, warning or conviction for an indictable offence fell from 33,700 to 23,300, a decline of almost 31 per cent. A possible source of the misconception is that while girls' detected offending was falling, the number convicted at court rose sharply from 4,200 to 6,000. The divergence between the two trends is explained by a relative reduction in the use of pre-court disposals, generating a higher level of prosecution: the proportion of girls' offending resulting in a reprimand, final warning, or, prior to June 2000, a caution declined from 88 per cent in 1992 to 72 per cent a decade later. No doubt the increased visibility associated with such a rapid expansion in the female court population has contributed to the perception that girl's offending is a greater concern than hitherto.

Since 2003, there has been a growth in girls' detected offending, coinciding with the introduction of the sanction detection target. The increase is considerably sharper than that for boys. In 2007, girls' detected offending was 35 per cent higher than in 2003; the equivalent rise for boys was 16 per cent. The chart in Figure 2.4 (opposite) illustrates this point.

Again, this pattern is more likely to reflect a reduced use of informality in responding to girls' misbehaviour rather than a sudden expansion in offending by that group.

Race

The youth justice system has long been characterised by the over-representation of black and minority ethnic young people. Children classified as black or black British are less likely to receive a pre-court disposal, more likely to be remanded

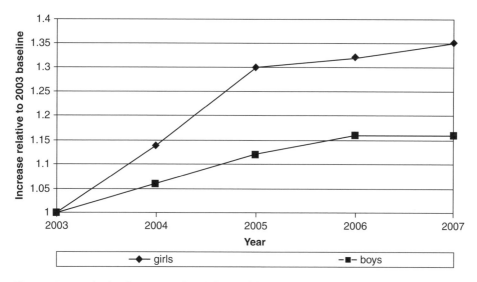

Figure 2.4 Relative increases in girls' and boys' detected offending, 2003–07

Source: NACRO (2009)

to custody or secure accommodation and disproportionately represented among those receiving a custodial sentence. During 2007–08, for instance, while black or black British young people made up 3 per cent of the general 10–17 population, they accounted for 7 per cent of those coming to the attention of the youth justice system, 14 per cent of those receiving a custodial sentence and almost one in three of those given a sentence of long-term detention (NACRO, 2009).

The Home Affairs Committee in its extensive inquiry into young black people and the criminal justice system concluded that the primary cause of such over-representation was social exclusion. However, the Committee also found evidence of discriminatory treatment by the youth justice system and noted elements within the black community itself – such as a lack of positive adult male role models – that might compound the negative impact of socio-economic disadvantage.

PRACTICAL TASK

Go to the Ministry of Justice report 'Statistics on Race and the Criminal Justice System 2008/09' (available at www.justice.gov.uk/stats-race-and-the-criminal-justice-system-2008–09c1.pdf) and read the summary and chapter 3 ('Suspects; Stops and Arrests').

A number of explanations for the over-representation of BME individuals at various stages of the criminal justice system have been advanced. Write down what you think they might be.

PRACTICAL TASK (CONTINUED)

Once you have done this, look at the Equality and Human Rights Commission (2010) report on the operation of stop and search powers. Section 3 of the report provides a detailed discussion of various explanations for the disproportionate number of stop and searches undertaken on BME individuals and their feasibility ('Stop and Think; A Critical Review of the Use of Stop and Search Powers in England and Wales' available at www.equalityhumanrights.com/uploaded_files/raceinbritain/ehrc_stop_and_search_report.pdf)

The nature of youth offending

The majority of offences committed by young people are directed against property, despite a relative decline of such offending during the 1990s. In 2007, theft, handling stolen goods, burglary, fraud or forgery and criminal damage comprised more than 62 per cent of indictable offences committed by young people. Indeed, theft and handling offences alone represented almost half (46 per cent) of the total and accounted for the largest rise in detected youth crime over the previous 12 months. Violent offending, which understandably generates high levels of public concern, is by comparison less common and accounts for fewer than one in five (17 per cent) of indictable offences committed by children and young people. While offences of violence can, of course, be very serious in nature, it should not be assumed that all are. An analysis of this category suggests that a majority related to incidents towards the lower end of the scale of seriousness. During 2007, almost two-thirds of violent offending resulted in a reprimand or final warning, a higher proportion than for any offence type other than theft and handling stolen goods. In the recent period, concern over young people carrying knives has attracted considerable attention.

Robbery is another offence tending to generate the highest levels of public concern. It too has risen in the recent past, and the figures for 2007 show a slight increase for the third successive year. Nonetheless, robbery remains relatively rare, accounting for fewer than 1 in 20 indictable offences committed by young people.

Sexual offending likewise accounts for a very small proportion, less than 1 per cent, of the total volume of youth crime. Moreover, offences of a sexual nature fell – both in terms of absolute numbers and as a proportion of all indictable offences – during early 1990s and have remained relatively stable in the more recent period. As with violent offending, measured by outcome, many sexual incidents appear to be less serious than might be anticipated: in 2007, for instance, well over half (55 per cent) of such offences resulted in a pre-court disposal rather than prosecution.

If the majority of offences processed through the youth justice system are not towards the top end of seriousness, it is also the case that the large preponderance of serious crimes are committed by adults. During 2007, persons over the age of 18 years were responsible for almost four times as many violent offences and more than 5.5 times as many sexual offences as children and young people. Robberies were evenly distributed, with adults being responsible for half the total as shown in Table 2.1 (opposite).

Table 2.1 Analysis of selected serious offences by age of offenders, 2007

Offences	Children and young persons as offenders (per cent)	Adults as offenders
Violence against the person	23	77
Sexual offences	15	85
Robbery	50	50

Source: NACRO (2009)

CASE STUDY: KNIFE CRIME

Given the way that offences are classified, it is not possible to ascertain what proportion of those entering the youth justice system have been involved with knife-related offending. However, the Offending, Crime and Justice Survey (Roe and Ashe, 2008) confirms that carrying a weapon is far from commonplace. During 2006, just 4 per cent of children aged 10–17 indicated that they had carried a knife in the previous year. The MORI youth survey (Mori, 2008) shows a substantially higher level of knife carrying, with 17 per cent of young people in mainstream education admitting having carried a penknife in the past 12 months during 2008. However, that figure represents a significant decline from the response to the equivalent question in 2005 (24 per cent), and a third of respondents confirmed that the primary purpose for carrying a knife was for sporting or similar activity.

In part, this may be the impact of the Tackling Knives Action Programme (TKAP) phase 1 (Home Office, 2009) which aimed to reduce the carrying of knives, related homicides and serious stabbings among teenagers aged between 13 and 19 years in ten police force areas. This programme involved a number of interventions, involving approaches such as education and other preventative approaches such as stop and search.

Among the provisional findings of this programme were the following.

- *Stop and searches increased in all ten areas, and there was a reduction in the number of recorded offensive-weapon offences.*

- *TKAP sharp instruments 'all violence' offences decreased by 17 per cent for victims aged 19 and under. A lower reduction was noted for victims aged 20 years and over (8 per cent).*

- *The number of robberies where sharp instruments were the main weapon reduced by 13 per cent for victims aged 19 years and under compared with an 11 per cent increase for victims aged 20 years and over.*

Overall, the findings for this initiative are encouraging, suggesting that fewer young people are becoming victims of knife crime. However, this trend is not the way in which knife crime is being focused upon by the media, and this aspect will be discussed further in the chapter that looks at media depictions of young people, crime and disorder.

First-time offenders

The target to increase the number of sanction detections has effectively been replaced by a target to reduce the number of first-time entrants into the youth justice system. Whereas the previous performance measure provided an incentive to deal formally with behaviour that might otherwise have received an informal response, the logic of the latter indicator is precisely the opposite. One might as a consequence anticipate a future rise in the use of various informal measures or formal disposals that do not constitute first-time entry.

There is an increasing array of disposals available to young people who come to the attention of the police for offending behaviour prior to prosecution. In addition to the system of reprimands and final warnings introduced by the Crime and Disorder Act 1998, the police can deal with offending behaviour in the following ways.

- A penalty notice for disorder.
- A youth restorative disposal, currently available in eight pilot areas.
- Recording no further action in areas where there is a system of 'triage' in place that allows a process of diversion in appropriate circumstances following a Youth Offending Team assessment.
- A youth conditional caution, to be introduced later this year in selected pilot areas for 16- to 17-year-olds.

The first three of these options do not count as first-time entry, and an increased use of each might accordingly be anticipated in the coming period as decision making is increasingly directed towards meeting the new target.

Figures released by the YJB show that there was a fall in first-time entrants between March 2005 and March 2008, and these indicate that the target for a reduction of 5 per cent over that period had been exceeded. Separate figures published by the Department for Children, Schools and Families (DCSF) also confirm that the target was met. However, the latter data differ in certain respects from those provided by the Board. First, despite the fact that the DCSF figures relate to England alone, they are considerably higher than those released by the YJB. Second, whereas the Board's data show a fall in both the two years from April 2006, those published by the DCSF show a rise in the first year followed by a reduction in the most recent 12 months. Finally, the DCSF data give information over a longer period, demonstrating that, despite the recent fall, the number of first-time entrants is still high by comparison with earlier years.

Young people as victims of crime

Having discussed at some length the idea of young people as offenders and perpetrators of crime and disorder, the following section discusses young people in a different light – as victims of crime. This category of victim is often underestimated due to the perception that young people are instigators of deviancy rather than being also victims of criminal and anti-social behaviour activity.

Personal crime

The 2003 Crime and Justice Survey (Home Office, 2005) found that those in the younger age groups were the most likely to have been the victims of personal crime (assault, robbery, theft from the person and other theft of personal property) in the previous 12 months. About a third of 10- to 15-year-olds and 16- to 25-year-olds had experienced one or more personal crimes (at 35 per cent and 32 per cent, respectively, the differences being not statistically significant). The prevalence of personal crime was considerably lower among the 26–65 age group (at 14 per cent).

Victimisation remained at around the same high level between the ages of 10 and 19 (between 33 per cent and 38 per cent) before declining, but there was variation within the types of crime experienced.

Theft and robbery

The level of victimisation of theft from the person peaked among 18- to 19-year-olds (12 per cent) and that of robbery peaked among 16- to 19-year-olds (6 per cent). This compared with 6 per cent for theft from the person and 2 per cent for robbery for 10- to 11-year-olds (still above the proportion of those aged 26–65 who were victims). Those aged 10–11 years were the most likely to have been victims of other thefts of personal property, such as thefts from changing rooms, with 16 per cent reporting this during the previous 12 months (NACRO, 2009).

Among 10- to 17-year-olds, money was most frequently the target of thefts (28 per cent of victims). Mobile phones were the target for 25 per cent of victims, followed by stationery (20 per cent) and bicycles (11 per cent). There was considerable variation within the 10–17 age group in the items stolen (likely to be linked to different patterns of ownership). Those aged 10–11 years were significantly less likely to have mobile phones or bank cards stolen and more likely to have stationery stolen.

Assault

The proportion of 10- to 15-year-olds experiencing assaults (21 per cent) was slightly higher than that of 16- to 25-year-olds (19 per cent) although this difference was not statistically significant. Older adults were far less likely to have been victims of assault (7 per cent). Assaults among younger age groups are often assumed to be more trivial. While the highest prevalence of more serious assaults (those that resulted in injury) was among 18- to 19-year-olds (14 per cent), this was not significantly different from the proportion for 10- to 11-year-olds (11 per cent). Prevalence was relatively similar up to the ages of 20–21 and fell away significantly above that age.

Threats and criminal damage

In addition to the offences included in the 'personal crime' category, threats and criminal damage to personal property were also covered. Respondents were asked whether they had been threatened 'in a way that actually frightened' them. The level of threats was higher among the younger age groups (12 per cent for those aged 10–15 and 14 per cent for those aged 16–25) than among the age group of 26–65 (9 per cent). There were no significant differences between the younger age groups although the nature of threats may change. Criminal damage to personal property was about the same level for all age groups (4 per cent) although the target of the damage would be likely to change with patterns of ownership (NACRO, 2009).

Bullying

In addition to criminal victimisation, young people were also asked whether they had been 'bullied in a way that frightened or upset' them in the previous year and about the nature of these incidents (these may also have been recorded as crimes in the survey). Among 10- to 17-year-olds, 19 per cent said they had been victims of bullying. Those aged 10–11 were significantly more likely to be victims within this group (27 per cent compared with 9 per cent of 16- to 17-year-olds). Females were also more likely to experience bullying (21 per cent) than males (17 per cent). Just over half of those bullied (52 per cent) said it had involved face-to-face abuse or verbal offensiveness. Around a third (32 per cent) said it had involved a physical assault, and a fifth (19 per cent) said it had involved threats. Some of these incidents were, therefore, technically criminal in nature (it was not clear whether they were regarded as such by victims). It was not possible to calculate precisely the extent to which criminal incidents reported to the survey by young people were related to bullying. However, it is clear that only a proportion of criminal victimisation of young people is accounted for by bullying, as 59 per cent of victims of violent crime said they were not the victims of bullying.

Repeat victimisation

In addition to looking at the proportion of people who have been the victims of crime, the research also examined the extent to which individuals were repeatedly victimised. The highest level of repeat victimisation was within the violence categories (assault and robbery), and it was particularly high for the younger age group: 60 per cent of 10- to 15-year-olds who experienced violence in the previous 12 months did so on more than one occasion. A fifth (19 per cent) had experienced five or more violent incidents in the previous 12 months. Older age groups who had experienced violence were less likely to be repeat victims. Within the violence category, repeat victimisation was particularly common for assaults resulting in injury. Again, the youngest victims were most likely to experience more than one incident (43 per cent of 10- to 15-year-old victims were victimised more than once, 40 per cent of 16- to 25-year-olds and 30 per cent of those aged 26–65). Around a fifth (19 per cent) of victims aged 10–15 accounted for two-thirds (66 per cent) of all violent incidents in that age group.

CASE STUDY: VIOLENT CRIME PATTERNS IN SOMERSET

Between 2003–04 and 2004–05, violent crime figures in Somerset almost doubled. In contrast, other reported crimes (i.e., burglary and vehicle crime) had fallen markedly over the same period. As a result, the crime and disorder reduction partnership undertook research to understand the patterns in violent crime as part of their six-month strategic assessment. Crime data were looked at both spatially (in which area did the crimes occur) and temporally (at what time of day did crimes occur). The objective was to look beyond trends in the aggregate numbers and to uncover where there were crime concentrations or 'hotspots', uncover when in the day violent incidents occurred, establish the profile of victims and perpetrators and explain why the patterns observed in the analysis occurred.

The expectations were that violent crime would be focused around domestic abuse, hate crime and the night-time economy violence, a pattern that was subsequently largely confirmed. However, there was a surprise. Over Somerset as a whole, four drivers of violence were identified: youth violence (which accounted for 27 per cent of recorded incidents), night-time economy violence (23 per cent), domestic abuse (22 per cent) and hate crime (3 per cent).

The most surprising finding was the level of violence linked to young people. Much of the violence seen in the daytime involved young people on weekdays between 3 and 5 pm, associated with the end of the school day. Victims tended to be 14 years old. It was observed that there were strong links to bullying, criminal damage, anti-social behaviour and robbery. The hotspots in Somerset occurred in most town centres in the county and coincided especially with areas shown to have higher levels of deprivation.

(www.creatingexcellence.org.uk/regeneration-renewal-article228-p1.html)

Patterns and risk factors

Just as those who come into contact with the criminal justice system as offenders have been found to have statistically similar characteristics, so too can this approach be applied to young people who become victims of crime. For example, some of the variations discussed above between the younger age groups are likely to be driven by their fast-changing situation as Finkelhor and Hashima (2001) point out. Changes in physical size will play a part in changing the nature of incidents they experience or do not experience. As they grow, young people become progressively less dependent and are less likely to experience the particular types of crime that are related to dependency (in particular, crimes of maltreatment). In parallel with this change, there is usually a reduction in guardianship and an increasing exposure to lifestyles that will put young people at higher risk of other types of crime (for instance, robbery). In addition, the changing value and status of personal belongings is also likely to play a part. Further, other factors that are related to the risks for young people of being victims of crime come into play. Before reading on, try the task below.

We have already asked you in this chapter to identify factors related to young people's involvement in crime. These 'risk factors' typically fell into four groups.

1. Family – including inadequate, harsh or inconsistent parenting.

2. School/education – such as low educational attainment, truancy or exclusion.

3. Community – including residence in areas with low community cohesion and easy access to drugs.

4. Individual/personal – such as being male, having an offending peer group, poor physical or mental health or misuse of alcohol or drugs.

PRACTICAL TASK

Now think about the risk factors that may be prevalent in young people becoming the victims of crime. Write down what you think they are and why they might apply. To what extent do they differ from the risk factors outlined above?

Personal characteristics, the type of area that people live in, aspects of their lifestyle and their upbringing all interact to produce different levels of risk. Differences in lifestyle may expose individuals in the same area and with the same demographic profile to different levels of risk through, for instance, bringing them into contact more frequently with offenders or situations where offending is prevalent. The types of behaviour include:

- noisy neighbours, teenagers hanging around, people sleeping rough, people being harassed in the street, people using or selling drugs and people being drunk or rowdy in public;

- whether school has clear rules, pupils hit teachers, teachers praise good work and easy to truant;

- whether parents praise, listen, treat fairly and want to know where young person is and whether parents often argue/fight with each other.

Underlying predictors of victimisation

However, it is not clear to what extent the apparently strong associations with lifestyle characteristics actually reflect a direct link with victimisation. As an example, drug taking may only be associated with victimisation because a third factor, such as the nature of a friendship circle, is driving both drug taking and victimisation. To understand more fully which factors are really important in victimisation, and therefore where interventions would be best directed, the risk factors which are predictive of victimisation independently of other factors need to be identified.

Offending behaviour and lifestyle

Committing a criminal offence in the previous year was the strongest predictor of personal crime victimisation among 10- to 15-year-olds (NACRO, 2009). The odds of being victimised for that group were 2.5 times higher than for those who had not offended, other things being equal. Those who had carried out at least one act of anti-social behaviour also had statistically significant higher odds of being victims, although this was a less strong predictor. This is consistent with the general findings from other studies (Aye Maung, 1995). There is interest in the literature in the possibility that the victimisation of young people leads to offending and offending to victimisation through the developmental process. However, rather than displaying this direct relationship, as the study reported here is cross-sectional and represents only one year, the association is likely to reflect shared risk factors between offending and victimisation.

Local area

The area, in terms of relative deprivation or whether urban, was not a significant predictor of personal crime victimisation. This is in line with findings elsewhere (Aye Maung, 1995). However, another measure of the local area, the perceived prevalence of anti-social behaviour, was the second strongest predictor. Those who said three or more types of anti-social behaviour were common in their area had odds of being victims of personal crime that were three times those of young people who said none were (other things being equal). This is consistent with Smith et al. (2001) who point out that levels of victimisation and delinquency tend to vary between neighbourhoods in parallel with each other.

C H A P T E R   S U M M A R Y

This chapter has highlighted the different trends in young people as offenders and, just as importantly, as victims of crime. Clearly, the young person as offender and victim is not a new concept, and we have seen the historical precedence for such behaviour and for the reactions to young people engaged in what can be defined as deviant behaviour. Understanding the risks associated with becoming a young offender and/or victim appears to be an important idea if society is to prevent more young people becoming part of these categories.

FURTHER READING

'*Folk Devils and Moral Panics: The Creation of the Mods and Rockers*'. A comprehensive account of the construction of moral panics is provided in Cohen's (1973) publication.

Detailed figures on the extent and nature of youth crime can be found in NACRO's (2009) youth crime briefing and various Home Office and Ministry of Justice publications: Hayward and Sharp (2005) '*Young People and Anti-Social Behaviour: Findings from the 2003 Crime and Justice Survey.*' Home Office Findings No. 245; Roe, S and Ashe, J (2008) '*Young People and*

Crime: Findings from the 2006 Offending, Crime and Justice Survey,' Home Office, London; Home Office (2005) '*The Victimisation of Young People: Findings from the Crime and Justice Survey 2003*' and Ministry of Justice (2007) '*Criminal Statistics 2006; England and Wales*'.

Reluctant Gangsters: Youth Gangs in Waltham Forest. An account of young people's involvement in gangs can be found in John Pitt's 2007 publication on youth gangs in North East London, available as a download at www.walthamforest.gov.uk/reluctant-gangsters.pdf

Clancy, A, Hough, M, Aust, R and Kershaw, C (2001) *Crime Policing and Justice: The Experience of Ethnic Minorities.* Home Office Research Study No. 223. London: Home Office.

Hackney Youth Offending Team (2009) *Pre-Court Disposals.*

Hayward, R and Sharp, C (2005) *Young People and Anti-Social Behaviour: Findings from the 2003 Crime and Justice Survey.* Home Office Findings No. 245. London: Home Office.

Ministry of Justice (2010) *Statistics on Race and the Criminal Justice System 2008/09: A Ministry of Justice Publication Under Section 95 of the Criminal Justice Act 1991.* London: Ministry of Justice.

Youth Justice Board (2004). *MORI Youth Survey 2004.* Available online at www.youth-justice-board.gov.uk/Publications/ (accessed 23 June, 2011).

Aries, P (1996) *Centuries of Childhood.* London: Pimlico.

Aye Maung, N (1995) *Young People, Victimisation and the Police: British Crime Survey Findings on Experiences and Attitudes of 12 to 15 Year Olds.* Home Office Research Study No. 140. London: Home Office.

Brown, S (1998) *Understanding Youth and Crime.* Buckingham: Open University Press.

Chesney, K (1991) *Victorian Underworld.* London: Penguin.

Cohen, S (1973) *Folk Devils and Moral Panics: The Creation of the Mods and Rockers.* London: Paladin.

Equality and Human Rights Commission (2010) *Stop and Think; A Critical Review of the Use of Stop and Search Powers in England and Wales.* Equality and Human Rights Commission.

Finkelhor, D and Hashima, P (2001) The Victimisation of Children and Youth: A Comprehensive Overview, in White, S (ed) *Handbook of Youth and Justice.* New York: Plenum Publishers.

Home Office (1989) *The Children Act.* London: Home Office.

Home Office (1999) *The Management of Health and Safety Regulations.* London: Home Office.

Home Office (2005) *The Victimisation of Young People: Findings from the Crime and Justice Survey 2003.* London: Home Office.

Home Office (2009) *Tackling Knives Action Programme (TKAP) Phase 1: Overview of Key Trends from a Monitoring Programme.* London: Home Office.

Loader, I, (1996) *Youth, Policing and Democracy*. Basingstoke: Macmillan.

McNeill, F (2002) *Beyond 'What Works': How and Why Do People Stop Offending?* Briefing Paper 5. Criminal Justice Social Work Development Centre for Scotland.

Ministry of Justice (2007) *Criminal Statistics 2006; England and Wales*, November 2007. London: Ministry of Justice.

Mori (2008) *Mori Youth Survey: Young People in Mainstream Education*. Available online at www.yjb.gov.uk/publications/Scripts/prodView.asp?idProduct=436&eP=

Muncie, J (2009) Youth, in Wakefield, A and Fleming, J (eds) *The Sage Dictionary of Policing*. London: Sage.

NACRO (2009) *Youth Crime Briefing*. London: NACRO.

Pearson, G (1983) Hooligan: *A History of Respectable Fears*. Basingstoke: Macmillan.

Pitts, J (2007) *Reluctant Gangsters: Youth Gangs in Waltham Forest*. Available online at www.walthamforest.gov.uk/reluctant-gangsters.pdf

Roe, S and Ashe, J (2008) *Young People and Crime: Findings from the 2006 Offending, Crime and Justice Survey*. London: Home Office.

Salgado, G (1999) *The Elizabethan Underworld*. Trowbridge: Redwood Books Ltd.

Smith, D, McVie, S, Woodward, R, Shute, J, Flint, J and McAra, L (2001) *The Edinburgh Study of Youth Transitions and Crime: Key Findings at Ages 12 and 13*. Edinburgh: University of Edinburgh.

Stewart, A, Dennison, S and Waterson, E (2002) *Pathways from Child Maltreatment to Juvenile Offending*, Griffith University. Available online at www98.griffith.edu.au/dspace/bitstream/10072/28177/1/57712_1.pdf

Webster, D (2006) Welfare reform: facing up to the geography of worklessness. *Local Economy*, **21**(2), 107–116.

USEFUL WEBSITES

www.asb.homeoffice.gov.uk/article.aspx?id=9118 (Youth Offending Teams)

www.homeoffice.gov.uk/rds/bcs1.html (British Crime Survey)

www.jrf.org.uk/ (The Joseph Rowntree Foundation)

www.nacro.org.uk/ (National Association for the Care and Resettlement of Offenders, NACRO)

www.ncvys.org.uk/ (The National Council for Voluntary Youth Services)

www.opsi.gov.uk/ (Office of Public Sector Information)

www.yjb.gov.uk/en-gb/ (Youth Justice Board)

3 Perceptions of young people

Introduction

This chapter examines perceptions of and by young people both historically and at the present time. It considers the extent to which current depictions of young people differ from portrayals of young people in the past and utilises the concept of moral panic to help understand the similarities. In particular, the chapter considers the way in which young people are depicted in the media and considers the extent to which this has impacted policy in relation to young people.

The chapter also considers the practical implications that have arisen as a result of the way young people have been demonised by the media and how this has influenced the way in which they have been policed. Additionally, the chapter considers the way in which performance measurements have impacted young people.

What do we mean by perception?

Very often we hear about how people feel about such things as the fear of crime. The term often used, particularly in research documents or official documents produced by governments and other agencies, refers to people's perception of the fear of crime or some such topic. The term is often used by politicians, academics and other people to help explain issues, and it appears that in general, perception relates to awareness of objects or situations, usually by our senses. A simple yet effective definition of perception is as follows:

> *Perception refers to the way in which we interpret the information gathered by the senses.*

> (Eysenk, 1993)

So it appears that we form perceptions and therefore opinions as a result of gathering information about a particular subject from a number of sources. One way in which we gather perceptions regarding a vast amount of issues including crime and disorder is through the media.

The role of media in forming perceptions

Crime and disorder occupies a large amount of media space as novels, TV shows, newspaper articles, comics and documentaries, including real-life reconstructions of criminal events through shows such as *Crimewatch*. It appears to have a fascination for people, and much of our perception regarding crime, disorder and the fear of crime comes through the secondary source of the media.

The type of crime the media report has remained constant over the years despite the fact that the amount of crime reported in newspapers has actually increased. Historically, the media appear to report specific types of crime which can lead to a distorted perception of the amount of the specific crime actually taking place. Research into this facet and the results obtained can be seen in Table 3.1.

Table 3.1 Research into reported crime

Research undertaken	Crime and percentage reported	Percentage of reported crime
Ditton and Duffy (1983), Strathclyde area	Violence and sex offences; 45.8% of newspaper coverage	2.4% of reported crime
Smith (1984), Birmingham area	Robbery and assault offences; 52.7% of newspaper coverage	6% of reported crime
Williams and Dickinson (1993), UK-wide national newspapers	Personal violence; 60% of newspaper coverage	6% of reported crime

Clearly, while the newspapers, in particular, and the media, in general, do inform the public, they can also help to create a public awareness that is substantially different from a 'reality' contained in victim surveys or in the official statistics.

The type of information the mass media select and disseminate to the public is tainted throughout by the notions of newsworthiness; rather than providing a pure reflection of the world, media select events that are atypical and present them in a stereotypical fashion and contrast them against a backcloth of normality which is over typical.

Therefore, using such an approach, criminals are usually shown as violent, immoral and a threat to an otherwise peaceful social order (Young, 1974).

Consequently, all forms of media are constantly searching for the new, the unusual and the dramatic to present to the public. In order to find 'news', Chibnall (1977) suggests that five informal rules of relevancy are applied and it is these that govern the professional imperatives of popular journalism.

Chibnall's rules of relevancy can be seen in Table 3.2 below

Table 3.2 Rules of relevancy

Rule of relevance
Visible and spectacular acts
Sexual or political connotations
Graphic presentation
Individual pathology
Deterrence and repression

Chibnall (1977) argues that media reports cannot simply be a reflection of real events because there are two key processes that are at work, namely that of selection (which aspects of events to report or omit) and presentation (choosing what sort of headline, film, photograph, etc. to use) Chibnall (1977) suggests that the violence most likely to receive coverage in the media is that which involves sudden injury to others especially in public places. Concern with such violence has typified media accounts throughout the past 50 years, supported by such media labels as 'bullyboy skinheads', 'vandals', 'thugs', 'hooligans', 'joy riders' and more latterly 'hoodies' and 'happyslappers'. The concentration on these forms in media and public discussions reinforces limited ideas concerning what types of crime are being committed and who commits them.

PRACTICAL TASK

Having considered the information above regarding the way media report crime and disorder, visit the website www.youtube.com/watch?v=pqyU2z-FJr8&feature=related which contains a news report entitled 'Manchester Hoodies/Scallies/Chavs/Thugs/Scrotes Gang'.

Once you have seen this video, consider the following questions.

- How representative of the young people of Manchester do you think these young people are?

- In which way have the youngsters in this video been presented by the media?

- What effect would this video have on people's perceptions of young people?

The application of stereotypes is a characteristic feature of most crime reporting. It tends to be presented in terms of a basic confrontation between the symbolic forces of good and evil, with complex social events being collapsed into simplistic questions of right or wrong. The intricate history and complex picture are rarely provided or considered. When looking at the video in the practical task box, consider how much of the complex social problems in this particular area are truly considered or reported upon.

Moral panic

'Moral panic' has been a term used by many to describe the public reaction (or more importantly, media and political reactions) to many aspects of our lives. It has been used to describe reactions to a number of events such as mugging, soccer violence, social security scroungers and more importantly youth sub-cultures and perceived youth deviance. Jewkes (2009) offers us this definition of moral panic:

> *A hostile and disproportional social reaction to a condition, episode, person or group defined as a threat.*
>
> (Jewkes, 2009, p 227)

The first systematic study of a moral panic in the United Kingdom was Cohen's (2002) research on the social reaction to the Mods and Rockers disturbances of 1964. Over the bank holiday that weekend, groups of working-class youths arrived in the seaside resort of Clacton. The holiday period was wet and cold, and shopkeepers were irritated by a lack of business, while facilities for young people were extremely limited. Eventually, scuffles broke out, and some windows were broken, beach huts vandalised and scooters and motor cycles driven at speed along the promenade.

A brief contextual video of these types of event can be seen at the following website: www.youtube.com/watch?v=r61ks18Bd7I

Such events were by no means new. A historical study of hooliganism in Britain by Pearson (1983) discovered many instances of similar behaviour. However, the difference between the historical events discussed by Pearson and the events of 1964 was that the Mods and Rockers incident received the undivided attention of the media with front-page coverage in the national press. These reports constrained phrases such as 'day of terror' and a mob 'hell bent on destruction', and youths were presented as being engaged in a confrontation between two easily recognisable groups.

However, Cohen's research did not discover any such structure among the groups, and the most common offence reported was threatening behaviour, not assaults or damage. Indeed, a few days later, a reporter admitted that the event had been over-reported (Cohen, 2002, p 31).

The point to note about this event is that it set in motion a train of events. These were as follows.

- It initiated a wider public concern that meant that the police had to be more vigilant.

- This resulted in more arrests, court appearances, fines, etc. which appeared to confirm media reaction.

- Because of this reaction, youths felt obliged to identify with one of the two groups.

- This process reinforced the original image and produced more clashes in several seaside resorts.

- This encouraged more media coverage, increased police activity and encouraged further public concern.

Wilkins (1964) produced a model which demonstrates how a deviancy amplification spiral can be set in motion. This can be seen in Figure 3.1 below.

The media's distortion of the initial events in 1964 resulted in an amplification of youthful deviance both in perceived and in real terms. Youths began to identify

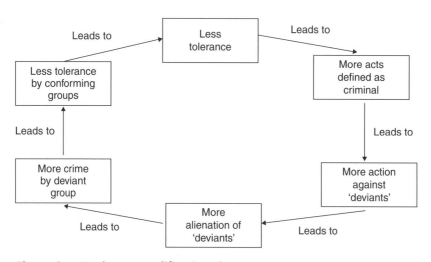

Figure 3.1 Deviancy amplification theory

with the label attached to them and as a result believed themselves to be more deviant and separate from the rest of society.

The moral panic approach not only helps us identify instances of media exaggeration and distortion but also maintains that selective reporting and police action can create crime waves and other social problems.

PRACTICAL TASK

Read the text below which was published in The Sun on 1 July 2008 and consider the questions posed after the text. The text refers to the murder of a youth in London.

VICIOUS hoodies chillingly warned, 'Were going to stab you' – weeks before he was knifed to death. Brave *** warned off the thugs when they tried to steal a mountain bike outside the net café where he worked part-time. His boss said they repeatedly returned, demanding to confront the schoolboy. He recalled: They were saying, Where is he? We're going to stab him? It was very frightening. I'm convinced the incidents are connected. *** didn't have any other enemies.*** colleague added: 'These troublemakers looked like typical hoodies'. *** was stabbed repeatedly in North London, early on Sunday. Two youths arrested were released on police bail yesterday. Police last night recovered two knives. One, a 3 in wooden-handled knife, was found in a drain yards from the murder scene. Seventeen teenagers have been murdered in London this year.

Having read the text, and in light of the discussion surrounding media presentation of youth, crime and moral panics, consider these questions.

- *What are considered to be typical hoodies?*

- *How are hoodies represented within this text?*

- *What evidence is presented in this report that connects this particular case with the fact that 17 other teenagers have been murdered in London?*

- *Can you apply elements of the deviancy amplification theory to these circumstances?*

We can see how media portrayals, especially of young people, help form negative stereotypes that influence perceptions. The media can influence not only our perceptions of young people but also official responses to dealing with young people. The following section will consider, by use of case studies, how perceptions of young people can influence society and responses to them.

The case of the hoodies

The hoodie culture is one that has often been cited as being a major problem in modern society. Youths who wear hoodie-style clothing are seen as synonymous with gangs, especially gangs believed to carry knives and therefore are to be treated with caution and to be regarded as inherently criminal. This stereotyping of young people, based on what they wear, can have an effect on the way in which they are able to carry on their daily lives.

CASE STUDY

Hooded tops, baseball caps and swearing have been outlawed at Bluewater shopping centre in Kent as part of a crackdown on anti-social behaviour. The retail and leisure complex is bringing in a zero-tolerance approach to intimidating conduct. The move has been backed by Kent Police which has a dedicated on-site team. Bluewater property manager, Helen Smith, said that the decision was taken because there had been 'issues' in the centre 'at certain times of the week'. Managers have drawn up a code of conduct for the centre, and people contravening it will be asked to leave the complex. The rules outline the standard of behaviour expected, including not smoking, leafleting or canvassing on site. Guidelines say intimidating behaviour by groups or individuals, anti-social behaviour including swearing and wearing clothing which deliberately obscures the face such as hooded tops and baseball caps, will not be allowed. Ms Smith said: 'We're very concerned that some of our guests don't feel at all comfortable in what really is a family environment. That's feedback from retailers, our own staff and from our on-site police force'. She said there were nearly 400 CCTV cameras at Bluewater which were being constantly monitored. North Kent Supt, Martin Hewitt, said: 'By clearly setting acceptable standards of behaviour, this code will allow staff and police officers to work together in maintaining the quality of experience for guests'.

Policy decisions such as the above are probably introduced for what seems good reasons, and in the creation of every stereotype, there is always a kernel of truth. However, the application of rules and regulations based on perceptions of stereotypes not only is wrong because it disadvantages people but may actually in some cases be illegal.

Loitering or youth presence

Many calls for police assistance appear to revolve around the presence of groups of youths at street corners or outside shop premises during evenings. Much of this may be called youth presence rather than youth annoyance, but sometimes the presence of youths can be intimidating for some people. There is no denying that there are occasions when groups of youths have caused disturbances and behave in an unruly manner. However, a response based on generalisations of youth is unfair and can lead to a disproportionate response.

CASE STUDY

The Mosquito or Mosquito alarm (see Figure 3.2 below) (marketed as the Beethoven in France and the Swiss-Mosquito in Switzerland) is an electronic device, used for solving loitering problems, which emits a sound with a high frequency. The newest version of the device, launched late in 2008, has two frequency settings, one of approximately 17.4 kHz (http://en.wikipedia.org/wiki/The_Mosquito – cite_note-0) that can generally be heard only by young people, and another of 8 kHz that can be heard by most people. The maximum potential output sound pressure level is stated by the manufacturer to be 108 decibels. The sound can typically only be heard by people below 25 years of age, as the ability to hear high frequencies deteriorates in humans with age (a phenomenon known as presbycusis).

The device is marketed as a safety and security tool for preventing youths from congregating in specific areas. As such, it is promoted to reduce perceived anti-social behaviour such as loitering, graffiti, vandalism, drug use, drug distribution and violence. In the United Kingdom, over 3,000 have been sold, mainly for use outside shops and near transport hubs. The device is also sold in Australia, France, Denmark, Italy, Germany, Switzerland, Canada and the USA.

The Mosquito has attracted controversy on the basis of human rights. Critics say that it discriminates against young people and infringes their human rights, while supporters argue that making the Mosquito illegal would infringe the human rights of shopkeepers who suffer business losses when 'unruly teenagers' drive away their customers. Mosquito distributors have said that they keep standards to ensure that the device is not abused, and Howard Stapleton who invented the device has asked European governments to legislate guidelines governing its use.

Figure 3.2 Mosquito alarms on a shop corner.

Portrayal of young people in comics

It is not only the visual or audio media that typically represent young people in a poor light. All forms of media tend to indulge in such an approach, including the written type. The following case study illustrates how young people are stereotyped in a different sort of media.

CASE STUDY: RAT BOY

Rat Boy is a fictional character in the British adult comic Viz. He is an extreme caricature of the juvenile delinquent and criminal underclass, who lives by theft, has a strong drug habit and defies the law as openly as his youth allows. Rat Boy's age is variable from under 12 to mid teens. He always wears a tracksuit and goes barefoot in all weathers; his appearance is deliberately rat like, with huge ears, a long nose, protruding front teeth and a scampering gait. He displays his irreverence by defecating everywhere, especially in the properties which he burgles.

The inspiration of his character is from that of the real-life career criminal Tommy Laws, who is nicknamed Spiderboy by the police and the media due to his habitual climbing onto roofs and high places in order to evade capture.

His dialogue normally consists of northern English slang and constant profanity, with long offensive tirades often shouted at his victims or the police; sometimes, however, he shows himself to be highly intelligent and articulate, such as when making confessions and implicating others.

Most of his adventures involve breaking and entering, vandalising a place and taking anything of value, and then usually either evading the law or getting off very lightly because he is a child. When arrested at one house which he ransacked, he is sent on a 'self-esteem building for young offenders' programme, which turns out to be a holiday in Spain (http://en.wikipedia.org/wiki/Rat_Boy – cite_note-Viz_ comic.7CViz_.23100–0). He was once subject to house arrest, enforced by electronic tagging on his ankle – unable to remove the tag, he gnaws his own leg off and hops outside to quickly rob several more houses. The primary motive for Rat Boy's constant burglary and thieving is to acquire money for buying drugs, such as cannabis, crack and even heroin, or strong drink.

Impact on policy

Representations such as those highlighted in this chapter support the idea that all young people are constantly committing criminal acts, have no social consciousness and are only concerned with self-preservation and drug taking. They further accentuate the belief that the criminal justice system is far too lenient with young people who are caught, released and commit further offences. In many cases, the perceptions put forward by media in relation to young people reflect the class divisions that still exist in our society. It is clear that during the last century, developments in the terminology used to refer to the working class have become increasingly negative and unconstructive, meaning that social class has become distinguished by taste, and more importantly, a perceived *lack* of taste (Adams and Raisborough, 2008, p 1173). In particular, young people have suffered from this approach. In many respects, media productions are often used in order to distance 'other' working classes from an upheld notion of middle-class respectability and can, as we have seen with the case of the Mods and Rockers in 1964, influence Criminal Justice policy. For example, on 28 March 2007, *The Guardian* reported the following 'justice plan' to be introduced by the then Labour Government.

> *A new-style '11-plus' to assess the risk every child in Britain runs of turning to crime was among a battery of proposals unveiled in Tony Blair's crime plan yesterday. The children of prisoners, problem drug users and others at high risk of offending will also face being 'actively managed' by social services and youth justice workers. New technologies are to be used to boost police detection rates while DNA samples are to be taken from any crime suspect who comes into contact with the police. The 'early intervention' approach is part of a package of proposals on security, crime and justice produced by Downing Street which underline the scale of criminal justice reform Mr Blair believes is still needed despite passing 53 law and order bills since he came to power in 1997.*

> *The shadow home secretary, David Davis, focused his criticism on the extension of the DNA database to any crime suspect and the early intervention plans for children. He described the proposal to assess every child for risk of offending as the 'nanny state gone mad' while he said the Conservatives would have 'great and grave concerns' about any extension of the DNA database. A Home Office spokeswoman said the universal checks on children would look at factors including attainment at school, truancy rates and substance abuse.*

From the wording of this report, Government policy at the time suggested that every young person in the country may be capable of committing criminal acts and that there is a 'scientific' response that can eliminate this problem.

PRACTICAL TASK

Read the report above regarding the so-called justice plan and consider the following questions.

- *What evidence is there that supports this approach would be successful?*

- *What consideration if any appears to have been given to the human rights of the young people themselves?*

- *Do you think this approach labels the children of all offenders as offenders themselves?*

- *Can this actually be the case?*

In fact, this approach may be in contradiction of the United Nations Convention on the Rights of the Child, adopted in 1989 (for more details, visit www.unicef. org/crc/).

Perhaps, the area where the greatest impact of the media in relation to how young people are perceived, and how policy has been influenced, is that of the Anti-Social Behaviour Order (ASBO). In particular, the idea of anti-social behaviour connected with the presence of groups of youths seemingly 'hanging about' on the streets and other public places. While ASBOs are covered more fully elsewhere in this book, they will be discussed briefly here to illustrate the impact on government policy that the media can exert.

Anti-Social Behaviour Orders

Despite the present government's review of the use of ASBOs, as Burney (2005) points out, the idea of the ASBO has great popular appeal, boosted by media publicity, and as the existence of the order became more widely known, great public pressure. In general, ASBOs tend to be used for 'incivilities' affecting public space. A definition of anti-social behaviour is provided by Section 1 of the Crime and Disorder Act 1998:

Anti-social behaviour is defined in law as a person acting in a manner which caused or was likely to cause harassment, alarm or distress to one or more persons not of the same household as himself.

This Act also introduced, therefore, the ASBO. Police and local authorities can apply to a magistrate for ASBOs which were augmented by the Anti-Social Behaviour Act (Home Office, 2003) which provided for dispersal orders. Penalty notices for disorder were introduced which covered a wide range of misbehaviour. Concern has been expressed, however, over the large number of ASBOs imposed on juveniles and young people. Some 40 per cent are imposed on 10- to 17-year-olds, and many receive custody for breach of ASBOs. Young people are perceived as the main perpetrators of anti-social behaviour. 'Youths hanging about', for example, comes top of a list of aggravation in the British Crime Survey and many local crime and disorder audits.

The most striking aspect of ASBO statistics, therefore, is the extent to which they have been applied to children and young people. The media have been keen to report stories about out-of-control children being controlled by such orders. Burney (2005, p 99) cites two cases in particular worthy of contemplation.

1. A 14-year-old boy from Nottingham who became the first person to be given custody for breach of an ASBO. It has now been decided by those involved in this case that the ASBO actually made things worse.

2. The so-called Terror Triplets from Gillingham, Kent, who breached ASBOs and were thought to have deserved a prison sentence, but who actually received supervision orders.

While media reaction was that these young people deserved to be incarcerated, the family backgrounds of both were similar, with difficulties from an early age with other criminally motivated children in the family. Consequently, the public feed on media representations of these children which exaggerate the specific cases to form a general demonisation of young teenagers. There is seldom any attempt to link children's anti-social behaviour with family needs, and the remedy for solving what are social service problems often turns into calls for punishment. The ASBO has provided a convenient behaviour for dealing with children and young people who are also considered a nuisance, and the wide powers attached to it have led to a large number of punishments for what appear to be trivial annoyance, as follows, for example.

- A child forbidden to use the word 'grass'.

- Children forbidden to wear hoodies.

- 10-year-old twins given ASBOs for looking through windows.

(Burney, 2005, p 99)

PRACTICAL TASK

Consider the ideas of moral panic and deviancy amplification theory discussed earlier in this chapter and apply them to the idea of ASBOs and young people.

- Why do you think young people are more likely to obtain an ASBO than others?

- What role has the media played in the way young people are perceived in this area?

CHAPTER SUMMARY

Clearly, representations of young people in the media tend to alter or influence our perceptions of young people generally. We have seen that the media are involved in a very selective process regarding what they decide to present as news and items of interest to the public at large. The influence of the media can present young people in a general light, and can influence the criminal justice system and the way the police respond to perceived threats, or moral panics. We should never underestimate the power that the media has to portray different groups in particular ways, and despite some high-profile individual cases, the generalisation that all young people are engaged in criminal and unlawful activities is a false one and should be considered by police and policy makers alike.

FURTHER READING

Ditton, J and Duffy, J (1983) Bias in the Newspaper Reporting of Crime News. *British Journal of Criminology*, **23**: 159–65.

Pearson, G (1983) *Hooligan: A History of Respectable Fears.* London: Macmillan.

Smith, S J (1984) Crime in the News. *British Journal of Criminology*, **24**: 289–95.

REFERENCES

Adams, M and Raisborough, J (2008) What can sociology say about Fair Trade? Reflexivity, ethical consumption and class. *Sociology*, **42**(6): 1165–82. Available online at http://soc.sagepub.com/cgi/reprint/42/6/1165 (accessed 17 July 2010).

Burney, E (2005) *Making People Behave: Anti-Social Behaviour, Politics and Policy: The Creation and Enforcement of Anti-Social Behaviour Policy.* Cullompton: Willan.

Chibnall, S (1977) *Law and Order News.* London: Tavistock.

Cohen, S (2002) *Folk Devils and Moral Panics: The Creation of the Mods and Rockers*, 3rd ed. London: Routledge.

Ditton, J and Duffy, J (1983) Bias in the newspaper reporting of crime news. *British Journal of Criminology*, **23**(2), 159–65.

Eysenk, M W (1993) *Principles of Cognitive Psychology.* Hove, UK: LBL Publishers.

Home Office (2003) *The Anti-Social Behaviour Act.* London: Home Office.

Jewkes, Y (2009) *Media and Crime.* London: Sage.

Pearson, G (1983) *Hooligan: A History of Respectable Fears.* London: Macmillan.

Smith, S J (1984) Crime in the news. *British Journal of Criminology*, **24**(3), 289–95.

Wilkins, L (1964) *Social Deviance.* London: Tavistock.

Williams, P and Dickinson, J (1993) Fear of crime: read all about it? *British Journal of Criminology*, **33**(1), 33–56.

Young, J (1974) Mass media, drugs and deviance, in Rock, P and McKintosh, M (eds.), *Deviance and Social Control.* London: Tavistock.

USEFUL WEBSITES

www.unicef.org/crc/ (UNICEF website).

www.youtube.com/watch?v=pqyU2z-FJr8&feature= (related website looking at Hoodies in Manchester).

www.youtube.com/watch?v=r61ks18Bd7I (website providing historical context for Mods and Rockers).

4 Anti-social behaviour and young people

Introduction

Attempts to tackle anti-social behaviour (ASB) formed a central plank of the Labour Government's criminal justice policy during its term in office (1997–2010). According to the Police Foundation, *the idea of antisocial behaviour as a distinctive problem requiring legislative and administrative solutions in its own right is a concept that has evolved in the past 15 years in Britain and is largely* associated with 'New Labour' (Police Foundation, 2010, p 1). In the preface to the Respect Action Plan (2006), the then prime minister, Tony Blair, described the problem of ASB as ... *a lack of respect for values that almost everyone in this country share – consideration for others, a recognition that we all have responsibilities as well as rights, civility and good manners* (Police Foundation, 2010, p 1).

CASE STUDY

A great deal of the recent public attention around the impact of ASB arose from the death of Fiona Pilkington and her daughter, Francesca, in October 2007, subsequently investigated by the Independent Police Complaints Commission (IPCC) in September 2009. The inquest into Ms Pilkington's death was told that she and neighbours had made 33 calls over a seven-year period asking police for help after suffering repeated and continuing abuse and torment from a gang of youths outside her home in Barwell, Leicestershire. Finally, Ms Pilkington drove to a lay-by near Earl Shilton, Leicestershire, on 23 October 2007 and set the car alight with her and her disabled daughter inside the vehicle.

IPCC commissioner, Amerdeep Somal, said:'This is an extremely distressing case about which there is understandably a great deal of public concern. It appears to be a case where sustained anti-social behaviour in a neighbourhood over a period of several years has contributed to a truly horrific and tragic outcome. It is a primary duty of the police to protect the public. Anyone, in any community, has the right to feel safe in their home and the right to expect that when they report nuisance, abusive or anti-social behaviour it is dealt with seriously by the police' *(www.ipcc.gov.uk/news/Pages/pr_290909_pilkington.aspx).*

The range of measures introduced by governments (particularly New Labour) in the past 20 years has had significant implications for justice and the rule of law, most significantly because they curtail the rights and freedoms of individuals while having criminal rather than civil penalties attached to them. This appears to be recognised by the coalition government, which criticised New Labour's sanctions – *there were too many of them, they were too time consuming and expensive and they too often criminalised young people unnecessarily, acting as a conveyor belt to serious crime and prison* – although the extent to which this speech marks a significant change in government policy remains unclear (May, 2010, discussed in more detail at the end of this chapter).

It is important to recognise that most types of behaviour identified by the Government as 'anti-social' are in fact already proscribed under criminal law (Police Foundation, 2010). Although previously such powers would be largely exercised through civil injunctions and abatement notices imposed by local government, *the real shift came ... in 1997, when the incoming Labour government began to bring in new measures for responding to a much wider range of behaviours considered 'antisocial' but not necessarily 'criminal'* (Police Foundation, 2010, p 3).

What is ASB?

Before proceeding any further, it is important to clarify exactly what is meant by ASB.

PRACTICAL TASK

Have a look at the typology of ASB presented in table 2.1 of the Home Office's (2004) report 'Defining and measuring anti-social behaviour' (Home Office Development and Practice Report 26, available online at http://rds.homeoffice. gov.uk/rds/pdfs04/dpr26.pdf). What do you notice about the range of behaviours that is listed?

As you will have seen from the exercise above, precise definitions of ASB are notoriously difficult to develop because of the range of activities covered by the term and because the extent to which these behaviours are defined as 'anti-social' is subjective. This difficulty is reflected in the definitions of ASB that are provided in existing government legislation and policy.

> *Anti-social behaviour is any activity that impacts on other people in a negative way, and the key to categorising behaviour as anti-social must be consideration of its impact on others.*
>
> *The term 'anti-social behaviour' includes a variety of behaviour covering a whole range of selfish and unacceptable activity that can blight the quality of community life. Other terms such as 'nuisance', 'neighbour disputes' and 'disorder' are also used to describe some of this behaviour.*
>
> (http://homeoffice.gov.uk – Overview of ASB)

Examples of ASB cited on the website include the following.

- Nuisance neighbours.

- Yobbish behaviour and intimidating groups taking over public spaces.

- Vandalism, graffiti and fly-posting.

- People dealing and buying drugs on the street.

- People dumping rubbish and abandoned cars.

- Begging and anti-social drinking.

- The misuse of fireworks.

- Reckless driving of mini-motorbikes.

(Home Office Respect Anti-Social Behaviour website)

A legal definition of ASB was provided by the Crime and Disorder Act 1998, which described ASB as *acting in a manner that caused or was likely to cause harassment, alarm or distress to one or more persons not of the same household* as the perpetrator (Home Office Respect Anti-Social Behaviour website).

Two issues are immediately apparent from this definition.

1. The definition covers a wide range of activities, of varying degrees of seriousness, some of which are criminal acts, others not.

2. That what defines ASB is the perception of the victim or complainant, not the view of the person committing the act.

When asked in a television interview to clarify the parameters of anti-social behaviour, as the then minister of state in the Home Office, Hazel Blears replied: 'It means whatever the victim says it means'' (Chakrabarti and Russell, 2008, p 313).

The scale of ASB

One of the difficulties in tackling ASB is getting a clear indication of how large the problem is, due to the problems in defining precisely which incidents fall under the heading, and the extent details of such behaviour are routinely collected. To try and overcome this, on 10 September 2003, the Home Office Anti-Social Behaviour Unit asked those local government and public service organisations in England and Wales who received direct, first-hand reports of ASB to count the number of reports they received. Sixty-six thousand reports were made to the more than 1,500 participating organisations. Describing this as a 'useful snapshot', the Home Office estimated costs on the day of the count as being £14 million, with the estimate for the annual costs of responding to ASB being a minimum of £3.4 billion (the latter figure excluding the personal and social costs suffered by victims and communities) (Police Foundation, 2010).

ASB and young people

The issue of whether the focus on ASB specifically targets young people is, in McIntosh's words, *a contested area* (2008, page 253). Certainly, the government was keen to stress that the aim of their policy was not to punish young people disproportionately. The executive summary of the government's 2008 Youth Crime Action Plan stated that the *vast majority of young people make a positive contribution to society. Their success should be recognised and praised. They should be given a say in what goes on in their area, how local issues are addressed and how services intended for them are delivered. But a minority of young people continue to blight their communities by breaking the law and behaving in an anti-social way* (COI, 2008, p 4).

However, these sorts of statements have not stopped commentators from suggesting that recent policy on ASB supports the view that young people are a group from which communities need protecting (see, for example, Hill and Wright, 2003; Squires and Stephen, 2005b; Hughes and Follett, 2006; Stephen, 2006, all cited in McIntosh 2008). *The introduction of a raft of new legislation to deal with this social problem has seen the creation of a variety of behaviour regulation instruments ranging from night curfews to the Anti-Social Behaviour Order (ASBO). However, alongside these new sanctions, one target group of such interventions is distinctly familiar: troublesome young people. Within the current political climate, youths identified as anti-social currently wear the mantle of society's contemporary folk devils* (McIntosh in Squires, 2008, p 239).

The broader consequence of this particular construction of the problem is that anti-social behaviour has become a convenient peg on which to hang generalised prejudices about young people and their activities which make restrictive policies popular (Burney, 2005, page 67, cited by McIntosh in Squires, 2008, page 240). This targeted focus towards anti-social youths led (initially at least) to them becoming the disproportionate recipients of new statutory and non-statutory interventions, such as the Anti-Social Behaviour Order (ASBO) and Acceptable Behaviour Contracts (ABCs); indeed, Morgan and Newburn suggest that the former was *designed, inter alia, with juvenile ASB in mind* (2007, quoted in Squires, 2008). In addition, McIntosh emphasises the way in which the media constantly links the term 'ASBO' with images of hooded adolescents (as already discussed in Chapter 3) and by doing so *consolidates the anti-social master status of such youths* (McIntosh, p 240 in Squires, 2008).

Moore (2008) describes the disproportionate impact of attempts to tackle ASB on 'street life people' (a group he defines as those living the majority of their time in the company of others in public places, *who perform the whole range of social and physical activities in public places, including those which are generally regarded as private and/or inappropriate,* are generally unwaged and are often dependent on drugs and alcohol). He suggests that such groups are identified as being problematic primarily because of their *visibility* (using a term first explicitly used by Slovic in 1992). This explains why the public tend to react to their perceived threat in a concerned manner, and, in comparison, show much less concern towards other (private) problems that might objectively be judged as more harmful (Moore, 2008). Slovic suggested that the visual impact of a threat played a significant part in public perceptions of risk, so where 'normal social interactions' (such as arguing, raised voices, laughter and socialising) were carried out in public in full view of passers-by, they were found threatening as a result.

While Moore advances this thesis in relation to his street-life population, he also suggests that *the theoretical insights gained here can equally be applied to understanding the treatment of other groups, such as young people, new migrants and Travellers* (Moore in Squires, 2008, p 179), groups who are also more likely to spend time congregating on the streets or in public places for a variety of cultural, social and economic reasons.

Support for this notion of young people being viewed as problematic because of their visibility can be found in Mackenzie et al. (2010) who undertook a systematic review of the drivers of perceptions of ASB (PASB). They concluded that there is *frequently a mismatch between the objective measurement of ASB and how residents perceive ASB* (Mackenzie et al., 2010, page iii). Their analysis suggested that there were two 'processes of interpretation' that caused this.

1. *People utilise the observation of a particular phenomenon (e.g. teenagers hanging around) as a 'shorthand' way to judge the level of disorder in an area.*

2. *PASB is linked to deeper seated anxieties about the state of society in general and qualities of the neighbourhood in particular.*

The reason why people make different interpretations of behaviour rests in social connectedness. The connectedness of an individual to both other users of particular spaces and particular types of ASB is important in their evaluation of whether that behaviour is problematic or not. In essence, the more we know of those we share space with (say a group of young people), the easier it becomes for us to assess whether they pose a threat to us. By implication, the greater the connectedness of an individual, the less likely they would be to interpret any given behaviour as problematic ASB (Mackenzie et al., 2010, p iii)

Consequently, in proposing tactics deemed effective in combating PASB, Mackenzie et al. (2010) mention the importance of public information strategies. One of the examples they cite is *fostering positive media relations (e.g. between the local authority and local newspapers) to encourage the dissemination of 'success stories' in tackling ASB, and positive stories about young people), and to discourage 'scare stories' and the misrepresentation of isolated or unusual instances of ASB as commonplace* (Mackenzie et al., 2010, p i).

The British Crime Survey and ASB

The extent to which the presence of young people has become an indicator of ASB is shown with reference to the various perceptual measures of levels of ASB utilised by the British Crime Survey (BCS). The Home Office's 2009 report on perceptions of crime and ASB states that the latter *cannot be measured in the same way as experience of crime; it is often not possible to specify who is the 'victim' or what is an 'incident'. As a result, the BCS has included questions on perceptions of ASB for a number of years, including questions about how much of a problem a range of different types of ASB are in the local area* (Moon et al., 2009, p 24). Answers to seven specific questions are used to create an overall index of high levels of perceived ASB. The respondent is asked *for the following things I read out, can you tell me how much of a problem they are in your area. By your area I mean within 15 minutes walk from here*. The seven problems mentioned specifically are as follows.

1. Vandalism, graffiti and other deliberate damage to property or vehicles.

2. People using or dealing drugs.

3. People being drunk or rowdy in public places.

4. Rubbish or litter lying around.

5. Noisy neighbours or loud parties.

6. Abandoned or burnt-out cars.

7. *Teenagers hanging around on the streets* (author's emphasis).

Clearly, what is significant here is that for the most important British measurement of levels of perceived ASB, teenagers 'hanging around on the streets' is a core component. There is no comment about the type of behaviour teenagers are engaged in (not the case with 'noisy' neighbours, or 'loud' parties); it is simply their presence in public areas that is deemed to constitute ASB.

Interestingly, the typology of ASB created by the Home Office Research Development and Statistics Directorate in 2004 did not contain a specific 'youth nuisance' category, for precisely these reasons. The report states that, while this was considered, *the decision was taken not to include a youth category in the typology as it was felt that anti-social behaviour should be defined by the nature of the activity, not the age of the perpetrator. It was also felt that a youth category would attract reports of young people 'hanging around' and, while it is recognised that a group of young people can appear intimidating to members of the public, gathering in a group is not in itself necessarily anti-social. Only when these groups engage in nuisance or threatening activities can their behaviour be considered as anti-social behaviour and it is then the nature of the activity that defines it as such* (Home Office, 2004, p 5).

Range of sanctions available to tackle ASB

Currently, the police and other agencies have many tools at their disposal to try and tackle ASB including warning letters and interviews, contracts and agreements, fixed penalty notices and penalty notices for disorder, parenting orders, individual support orders, noise abatement notices, injunctions, dispersal powers, ASBOs, 'crack house' closure orders and premises closure orders, possession proceedings and, ultimately, custody.

Obviously, the range of sanctions reflects the different types of behaviour that fall under the umbrella of ASB circumstances in which these sanctions are applied, although their extent and complexity have been criticised, most notably in July 2010 by the then home secretary. In launching a review of ASB, she suggested that existing sanctions were

> *too complex and bureaucratic – there were too many of them, they were too time consuming and expensive and they too often criminalised young people unnecessarily, acting as a conveyor belt to serious crime and prison.*

> *On top of this, their use varies hugely from area to area, with practitioners tending to focus on the handful they are most familiar with. And if the professionals don't understand them, then how on earth are the perpetrators of anti-social behaviour supposed to understand them?*

> (May, 2010)

A brief outline of the powers and sanctions available to the police and other agencies is provided below.

Dispersal of groups

Part 4 (s30–36) of the Anti-Social Behaviour Act 2003 enables a senior police officer to designate an area where there is persistent ASB and a problem with groups causing intimidation.

- The area could be as small as a cash point or shopping arcade or it could be as wide as a whole local authority area, as long as there is evidence of ASB.

- The local authority must also agree to the designation (part of the strategic work of Community Safety Partnerships).

- The decision to designate an area must be published in a local newspaper or by notices in the local area.

- The designation can last for up to six months and can be renewed if necessary.

The designated area must be clearly defined, usually by a description of the streets or roads bordering the area.

Dispersal orders

Within dispersal areas, the police and designated police community support officers (PCSOs) have the power to:

- disperse groups where the relevant officer has reasonable grounds for believing that their presence or behaviour has resulted, or is likely to result, in a member of the public being harassed intimidated, alarmed or distressed;

- direct individuals to leave the locality and may exclude them from the area for up to 24 hours;

- return young people under 16 home, if they are out on the streets and not under the control of an adult, after 9 p.m. if they are either:

  ❖ at risk or vulnerable from ASB, crime, etc., or

  ❖ causing, or at risk of causing, ASB.

REFLECTIVE TASK

Consider the powers that the dispersal order gives police officers and designated PCSOs. Can you identify any potential consequences that might suggest why the police are often reluctant to use this power?

In practice, research undertaken for the Joseph Rowntree Foundation into the use of dispersal orders found that while they provided some short-term relief and a 'window of opportunity' for longer term anti-ASB measures to be introduced, the police tended to use dispersal orders as a last resort, favouring 'dialogue and nego-tiation' instead to disperse crowds (Police Foundation, 2010). The same study also found that the use of dispersal orders could lead to ASB being displaced to other areas and, if implemented in isolation of other measures, could fail to resolve ASB in the long term.

Penalty/fixed penalty notices

Fixed penalty notices and penalty notices for disorder are both one-off fines issued for ASB.

- Fixed penalty notices generally deal with environmental offences such as litter, graffiti and dog fouling and can be issued by local authority officers and PCSOs.
- These notices can be issued to anyone over ten years.
- Penalty notices are not the same as criminal convictions. However, failure to pay the fine may result in higher fines or imprisonment.

Examples of offences for which a notice might be issued are littering, graffitiing, fly-posting and noise nuisance.

Penalty notices for disorder

Penalty notices for disorder are issued for more serious offences.

- These notices can be issued to anyone over 16 years.
- They were introduced to address low-level ASB, while also reducing police bureaucracy and paperwork.

Examples of offences where a penalty notice for disorder may be issued include intentionally harassing or scaring people, being drunk and disorderly in public, destroying or damaging property, petty shoplifting, selling alcohol to underage customers, selling alcohol to somebody who is obviously drunk and using fire-works after curfew.

Acceptable Behaviour Contracts

ABCs, also known as an acceptable behaviour agreements, are interventions designed to engage the individuals in recognising their behaviour and its negative effects on others in order to stop the offending behaviour. An ABC is a written agreement between an ASB perpetrator and the local authority, Youth Inclusion Support Panel, landlord or the police.

- ABCs are usually used for young people but can also be used for adults.
- ABC consists of a list of anti-social acts that the offender agrees not to continue and outlines the consequences if the contract is breached.

- Contracts usually last for six months but can be renewed if both parties agree.

- ABCs are not legally binding but can be cited in court as evidence in ASBO applications or in eviction or possession proceedings.

Anti-Social Behaviour Order

ASBOs were introduced under the 1998 Crime and Disorder Act. They became available to the police and local authorities in April 1999 and are civil orders, made by a court, used to protect the public from behaviour that causes harassment, alarm or distress, but where criminal proceedings are inappropriate. Home Office guidance described the ASBO as being the final stage in a structured (and increasingly severe) approach to ASB that might previously have involved the use of warning letters, mediation or ASB contracts (Brookes, 2006).

ASBOs forbid specific threatening or intimidating actions. They can ban a person from:

- committing threatening, intimidating or disruptive actions;
- spending time with a particular group of friends;
- visiting certain areas.

The case study below gives an example where an ASBO has been made to prevent a young person entering certain areas.

CASE STUDY

ASBO youth gets five-county ban

A Nottingham teenager has been given an Anti-Social Behaviour Order (ASBO) banning him from five counties.

Nottingham Magistrates' Court heard how Scott Newbold, aged 16 and from Aspley, had terrorised members of the community with a gang of five other youths.

Among the incidents cited was one in which Newbold rode a motorbike into a community support officer.

Newbold has been banned from causing harassment in Notts, Lincs, Leics, Derbys and South Yorkshire.

Good news

The teenager has also been banned from being present in a vehicle without permission from the authorised keeper or driver, entering Broxtowe Country Park, in Nottinghamshire, and associating with certain individuals.

If he breaks the terms of the three-year ASBO which started on Tuesday, Newbold could face two years in prison.

(http://news.bbc.co.uk/1/hi/england/nottinghamshire/6199578.stm)

ASBOs are in effect for a minimum of two years and can be longer. They are designed to protect specific victims, neighbours, or even whole communities from behaviour that has frightened or intimidated them, or damaged their quality of life. It is important to note that they are civil orders – not criminal penalties – so they do not appear on a suspect's criminal record. However, if that person breaches an ASBO, they have committed a criminal offence, which is punishable by a fine or up to five years in prison.

A number of agencies can apply for an ASBO.

- Local authorities.

- Police forces.

- Registered social landlords and housing action trusts.

Use of ASBOs

> *PRACTICAL TASK*
>
> *Go to the Home Office website (http://rds.homeoffice.gov.uk/rds/antisocial1.html) and have a look at the details of the number of ASBOs issued up to the end of 2008. What do you notice about the numbers of ASBOs that have been issued?*

Initially *take up* [of ASBOs] *was slow. The cumbersomeness … and the cost of taking such proceedings discouraged many authorities from taking such action although their use subsequently increased* (Brookes, 2006, p 41). Overall, between April 1999 and December 2008, there were 16,999 ASBOs made in England and Wales. Of these, the age of the recipient was known for 16,691, 40 per cent of which (6,747) were made on young people aged under 18 (Ministry of Justice, 2010). The number of ASBOs in a full year peaked at 4,122 in 2005 before declining in each subsequent year to 2,027 in 2008 (Ministry of Justice, 2010). Table 4.1

Table 4.1 *ASBOs given to those aged 10–17 (number and percentage this represents of all ASBOs where age known)*

Year	Number (per cent)
2001	193 (56)
2002	251 (60)
2003	628 (47)
2004	1,340 (39)
2005	1,581 (39)
2006	1,053 (39)
2007	920 (40)
2008	719 (36)

Ministry of Justice (2010)

49

shows the percentage of ASBOs given to those aged under 18 in the period between 2001 and 2008 where the age of the recipient is known.

Again, the issue as to whether ASBOs are used disproportionately against the young is a matter of debate. Based on data up to the end of 2005, McIntosh recognises that the number of ASBOs issued to young people (those aged between 10 and 17) was less than the number issued to adults, and that over the same period the proportion of youth to adult ASBOs had declined year on year. However, he suggests that this analysis does not take account of the fact that the age range for young people (7 years) covered a much shorter period than the age range for adults. He also mentions the degree of regional variation that existed, so that in Greater Manchester, 51 per cent of ASBOs were issued to young people compared with 31 per cent in Greater London. He concludes *it is therefore wholly legitimate to argue that such orders remain disproportionately targeted at the youth age group* (McIntosh, 2008, footnotes 253–254).

McIntosh (2008) also mentions that the period between 1999 and 2005 had seen an increase year on year in the absolute *number* of ASBOs issued to those aged 10–17, although Table 4.1 shows that this pattern changes after 2005. Since then there has been a decline in the number of ASBOs given to young people (this decline is part of a more general decrease in the use of ASBOs, so the proportion of all ASBOs that they represent stays constant at around 40 per cent).

What does seem clear is that young people are more likely to breach ASBOs they receive than are adults. A comparison of the proportion of ASBOs that were breached between 1 June 2000 and 31 December 2008 shows that 65 per cent of orders made on those aged between 10 and 17 were breached compared with 49 per cent of those made on individuals aged 18 or over. These overall breach figures also mask some marked regional variations; the percentage of ASBOs breached for those aged between 10 and 17 ranged between 45 per cent (Suffolk) and 86 per cent (Dorset), while for those aged 18 or over, the range was between 34 per cent (South Wales) and 65 per cent (Dorset) (Ministry of Justice, 2010).

Of those breaching ASBOs between 1 June 2000 and 31 December 2008, those aged 10–17 were more likely to receive a community disposal and less likely to receive custody than those aged 18 or over (45 per cent of those aged 10–17 who breached ASBOs received a community sentence and 41 per cent were given custody compared with 16 per cent and 60 per cent, respectively, of those aged 18 or over). However, those in the 10–17 age group given custody were given a longer average sentence than those aged 18 or over (6.4 months compared with 4.9 months) (Ministry of Justice, 2010).

The high proportion of ASBOs that are breached, particularly by the young, has also led to claims that they are not proving effective as deterrents of ASB (Youth Justice Board, 2006). Indeed, the claim has been made that the receipt of an ASBO has become 'a badge of honour' among certain groups (Youth Justice Board, 2006). A review by the Youth Justice Board (2006) also suggested that many young people did not understand the terms of their ASBOs, which could result in many people breaking them. Others were just not prepared to accept the biggest restrictions on their lifestyles, such as hanging out with their friends.

As early as 2002, Home Office research found that among the 60 per cent of recipients of ASBOs where the data were available, *there was a high proportion where some mitigating factor appeared to have contributed to their behaviour. Almost a fifth had a drug abuse problem and a sixth a problem with alcohol. Problems with school were also common, with many being either temporarily or permanently excluded, or noted as having learning disabilities* – although the research did go on to say it was unclear in which way causality lay – *some of the problems may have been caused by their anti-social behaviour rather than being the cause of it* (Campbell, 2002, p 17). Similarly, a survey of youth offending teams published in 2005, which asked staff how many ASBOs made on those aged under 17 involved children with a diagnosed mental health disorder or an accepted learning difficulty, found the figure was over a third (35 per cent). Youth offending team staff were also asked in what proportion of these cases there had previously been an ABC (81 per cent; BIBIC, 2005, p 6).

Together and Respect Campaigns

Evidence of the recognition of the need to address some of the underlying causes of ASB and the lack of balance between enforcement and support had been explicitly recognised by the House of Commons Committee of Public Accounts (Police Foundation, 2010). The subsequent stages of the Labour administration saw a movement towards addressing the causes of ASB, particularly with the introduction of the Respect Campaign in 2006, and the accompanying Respect Action Plan (Police Foundation, 2010).

The Respect Campaign adopted an approach to ASB described as *broader, deeper* and *further*. 'Broader' meant addressing ASB in *every walk of life* (mentioned were school discipline and attendance, unacceptable behaviour by tenants and home owners and ensuring that public sector workers *respect the people they serve*). 'Deeper' meant *tackling the causes of disrespectful behaviour* (intervening in families with problems, providing support for parents, ensuring parenting classes were taken up, tackling drug and alcohol problems and *making sure that children and young people (were) active and learning how they can make their own contribution to our national life*). Finally, 'further' encompassed the introduction of more sanctions so *that everyone sees and expects a robust response to anti-social behaviour* (COI, 2006, p 7).

The coalition government and ASB

Statements from the coalition government in July 2010 appeared to mark a shift away from the previous government's policies, although the exact direction of the shift, and its consequences, is unclear at the time of writing. Under the heading 'Moving Beyond the ASBO', the home secretary, Theresa May, criticised Labour policy.

> *They knew they had to do something, but as with so much they did, their top-down, bureaucratic, gimmick-laden approach just got in the way of the*

police, other professionals and the people themselves from taking action. Such a centralised approach, imposed from Whitehall, can never be the best way to deal with an inherently local problem. Rather than part of the solution, the previous government's focus on anti-social behaviour became part of the problem.

(May, 2010)

In dealing with ASB, the police needed to be 'more responsive, active and account-able'. In the past *the police and the other agencies involved in tackling anti-social behaviour at local level took their cue from central government rather than the people they were meant to be serving*. There was a need to *replace bureaucratic accountability with democratic accountability (*May, 2010*)*.

May's speech criticised existing sanctions as 'too complex and bureaucratic'. *For 13 years, politicians told us that the government had the answer; that the ASBO was the silver bullet that would cure all society's ills. It wasn't. Life is more complex than that. That is why I have launched a review of the anti-social behaviour powers available to the police. I am determined to give them and the other agencies a toolkit that is appropriate and effective; with tools that are quick, practical and easy to use* (May, 2010). Overall, there was a need for *simpler sanctions, which are easier to obtain and to enforce, [and] will provide the police and practitioners with a firm hand to tackle the problem cases* (May, 2010).

C H A P T E R S U M M A R Y

Theresa May's speech was widely reported in the media as marking the death of the ASBO, a move confirmed by the terms of the government's review of ASB sanctions in February 2011 (Home Office, 2011). However, it would perhaps be a mistake to interpret the speech as marking a fundamental alteration of govern-ment policy with regard to ASB. Notwithstanding May's efforts to differentiate her government's intentions from those of its predecessor, there is much in her speech which maintains the previous administration's focus on ASB.

The speech opens by declaring *some people seem to believe anti-social behaviour is just a bit of a nuisance – a fact of modern life – but I believe it is time for us to stop tolerating it. Anti-social behaviour ruins neighbourhoods and can escal-ate into serious criminality, destroying good people's lives* (May, 2010). Although depicted as a new departure, the speech's continued emphasis on the general unacceptability of ASB, the importance of partnership and joined up working and the need for local solutions and community engagement in addressing ASB would all sound familiar to those involved in tackling ASB under New Labour.

The government's review suggests that there will be changes in the sanctions and powers available (with ASBOs being replaced by Criminal Behaviour Orders and Crime Prevention Injunctions [Home Office, 2011]). However, it seems unlikely that ASB will slip down the list of priorities that the police and other agencies are called upon to tackle. Support for this view is further provided by the research undertaken by Her Majesty's Inspectorate of Constabulary (HMIC) in 2010 which was highly critical of the service provided by the police to victims of ASB. Published in September 2010, shortly after May's comments, under the unequivocal title 'Anti-Social Behaviour; Stop the Rot', the HMIC report opined *we need a new start* (HMIC, 2010, p 3). While acknowledging there had been a great deal of effort to tackle ASB, and that the issue had had a high public profile in recent years, the report suggested that *ASB does not have the same status as 'crime' for the police. There are consequences to this* (HMIC, 2010, p 3).

The report suggested that *to fully understand the damage ASB causes we should take account of the victim perspective* (HMIC, 2010, p 5) and recommended the adoption of:

> an **early intervention strategy** (emphasis in document), similar to those in health and education sectors. It will require reform of police availability and a refocusing on what causes **harm** in communities, rather than what is or is not a 'crime', or what can be managed out of police systems. Make no mistake, it requires feet on the street.
>
> (HMIC, 2010, p 11)

However, it was clear that HMIC were not advocating a downgrading of the importance of tackling ASB, as the report made explicit:

> Confronted by spending cuts, some police chiefs and Community Safety Partnership members may be tempted to reduce the amount of work they do in relation to ASB and to concentrate instead upon volume crime. All the evidence we have available indicates that this would be a very significant mistake. Managing ASB is crucial to sustaining the vitality and confidence of communities. Untreated ASB acts like a magnet for other crime and disorder problems and areas can quite easily tip into a spiral of economic and social decline.
>
> (HMIC, 2010, p 12)

However, the implications of this 'refocusing' for young people are less clear and suggest that in certain respects, nothing has changed, as a final quote from the report demonstrates:

> Most importantly, individuals and communities must mobilise their defences by re-establishing acceptable rules of behaviour for those in public spaces or impacting on their neighbours, for example, **youths who congregate in town centre streets on Friday evening** (author's emphasis); drunks who habitually urinate in shop doorways; aggressive driving in residential streets.
>
> (HMIC, 2010, p 11)

FURTHER READING

A useful summary of the issues around ASB is contained in the Police Foundation's (2010) briefing on the subject. More detailed consideration of the impact of attempts to tackle ASB is provided in Squire's (2008) book *ASBO Nation: The Criminalisation of Nuisance*, particularly the chapters by Goldsmith, Moore and McIntosh. Details of the Labour Government's policies on ASB and the Respect Agenda can be found on the Respect website which provides details for practitioners of the sanctions available to tackle ASB (now archived to http://webarchive.nationalarchives.gov.uk/20100418065544/asb.homeoffice.gov.uk/article.aspx?id=9066). Theresa May's speech 'Moving Beyond the ASBO' can be found on the Home Office website at www.homeoffice.gov.uk/media-centre/speeches/beyond-the-asbo, and details of the proposed ASB review at www.homeoffice.gov.uk/publications/consultations/cons-2010-antisocial-behaviour/asb-consultation-document?view=Binary

Goldsmith, C (2008) Cameras, Cops and Contracts: What Anti-Social Behaviour Management Feels Like to Young People, in Squires P (ed) *ASBO Nation: The Criminalisation of Nuisance*. Bristol: The Policy Press.

REFERENCES

BIBIC (2005) *'Aint misbehavin' Young People with Learning and Communication Difficulties and Anti-Social Behaviour*. Available online at www.psychminded.co.uk/news/news2005/nov05/bibiccampaignupdate.pdf (accessed 31 January 2011).

Brookes, S (2006) Local authorities, Crime Reduction and the Law, in Moss K and Stephens M (eds) *Crime Reduction and the Law*. London and New York: Routledge and Taylor and Francis Group.

Campbell, S (2002) *A Review of Anti-Social Behaviour Orders*. Home Office Research Study 236. London: Home Office. Available online at rds.homeoffice.gov.uk/rds/pdfs2/hors236.pdf

Chakrabarti, S and Russell, J (2008) ASBOmania in Squires P (ed) *ASBO Nation: The Criminalisation of Nuisance*. Bristol: The Policy Press.

COI (2006) *Respect Action Plan*, Respect Task Force, January 2006.

COI (2008) HM Government Youth Crime Action Plan.

Her Majesty's Inspectorate of Constabulary (2010) *Anti-Social Behaviour; Stop the Rot*. London: HMIC.

Home Office (2004) *Defining and Measuring Anti-Social Behaviour*. Home Office Development and Practice Report 26. London: Home Office.

Home Office (2011) More Effective Responses to Anti-Social Behaviour. London: Home Office. Available online at www.homeoffice.gov.uk/publications/consultations/cons-2010-antisocial-behaviour/asb-consultation-document?view=Binary

Home Office Respect Anti-Social Behaviour Website. Now archived but available online at http://webarchive.nationalarchives.gov.uk/20100418065544/asb.homeoffice.gov.uk/article.aspx?id=9066

Independent Police Complaints Commission (2009) 'IPCC to investigate Leicestershire Police's response to Fiona Pilkington's calls for assistance'. Details of the progression of the IPCC investigation are available on the IPPC website at www.ipcc.gov.uk/news/Pages/pr_160310_pilkingtonupdate2.aspx

Mackenzie, S, Bannister, J, Flint, J, Parr, S, Millie, A and Fleetwood, J (2010) *The Drivers of Perceptions of Anti-Social Behaviour.* Home Office Research Report 34. London: Home Office.

May, T (2010) *Moving Beyond the ASBO* (Speech at Coin Street Community Centre, 28 July 2010). Available at HO website www.homeoffice.gov.uk/media-centre/speeches/beyond-the-asbo

McIntosh, B (2008) ASBO Youth: Rhetoric and Realities, in Squires P (ed) *ASBO Nation: The Criminalisation of Nuisance.* Bristol: The Policy Press.

Ministry of Justice (2010) *Statistical Notice: Anti-Social Behaviour Order (ASBO) Statistics England and Wales 2008.* Summary and data tables available from the HO website at http://rds.homeoffice.gov.uk/rds/antisocial1.html

Moon, D (ed), Alison Walker, A (ed), Murphy, R, Flatley, J, Parfrement-Hopkins, J, and Hall, P. (2009) *Perceptions of Crime and Anti-Social Behaviour: Findings from the 2008/09 British Crime Survey.* Supplementary Volume 1 to Crime in England and Wales 2008/09. Home Office Statistical Bulletin.

Moore, S (2008) Street life, neighbourhood policing and 'the community' in Squires P (ed) *ASBO Nation: The Criminalisation of Nuisance.* Bristol: The Policy Press.

Police Foundation (2010) *The Briefing; Antisocial Behaviour,* series 1, edition 9. London: Police Foundation.

Slovic, P (1992) Perceptions of Risk: Reflections on the Psychometric Paradigm, in Krimsky S and Goulding D (eds) *Social Theories of Risk.* Westport, CT: Praeger.

Squires, P (Ed) (2008) ASBO Nation: The Criminalisation of Nuisance. Bristol: The Policy Press.

Youth Justice Board (2006) Anti-social behaviour orders.

USEFUL WEBSITES

http://webarchive.nationalarchives.gov.uk/+/www.homeoffice.gov.uk/anti-social-behaviour/penalties/penalty-notices/ (ASB sanctions).

www.hmic.gov.uk/PROGRAMMES/ANTISOCIALBEHAVIOUR/Pages/home.aspx (HMIC website, details of overall research on ASB, reports for individual police forces, and links to the Universities Police Science Institute research).

www.homeoffice.gov.uk (Home Office website).

5 Young people and the criminal justice system

Introduction

Typically, systems of youth justice are beset by the ambiguity, paradox and contradiction of whether young offenders should be cast as 'children in need of help, guidance and support' or as 'corrupt, undisciplined and evil beings' who fully deserve their 'just desserts'.

(Muncie, p 143, in Hughes et al. 2002)

Welfarism has never been universally accepted as the best way of preventing youth crime. A strong law and order lobby has also ensured that a range of punitive custodial options (borstals, detention centres and youth custody centres) have remained in existence (Muncie, p 145, in Hughes et al. 2002). *It is generally accepted that a 'third way' in youth justice has emerged in the United Kingdom* (Newburn, 2002, p 559); Pratt (1989) develops this under the term 'corporatism', which embraces efficient and effective management of the offending population (Newburn, 2002, p 559), a centralisation of policy, increased government intervention and increasingly homogeneous aims shared by different professional groups (Pratt, 1989, p 245). As Burnett and Appleton (2004, p 34) suggest, the main argument in favour of a joined-up youth justice system is *that offending by children and young people is linked to a range of problems traditionally dealt with by separate agencies* (Waters, 2007, p 636).

From the 1990s, there has been a change in the tenor of official concern about juvenile offending, what Newburn describes as the *rediscovery of populist punitiveness* (2003, p 201; Joyce, 2006). This arose largely as the result of the urban disturbances of 1991, in Cardiff, Oxford, Tyneside, which occurred as a consequence of police efforts to prevent public displays of 'joyriding' (Campbell, 1993). These disturbances led to a reassertion by subsequent governments of the position of custody in the range of sanctions available to deal with young offenders (Joyce, 2006).

Youth justice under New Labour

This trend continued under the New Labour Government when it came to power in 1997, as illustrated by Tony Blair's infamous quote while shadow home secretary about the need to be 'tough on crime, tough on the causes of crime'. While in opposition, New Labour had begun to develop an approach to criminal justice policy combining elements of communitarianism, managerialism and populist punitiveness (Newburn, 2003). The party's proposals for reform of the Youth Justice System were contained in the 1996 paper 'Tackling Youth Crime, Reforming Youth Justice', which made it clear that this was a priority area for government. This document coincided with the Audit Commission report 'Misspent Youth' which provided a critical review of existing arrangements for young offenders. One of the main criticisms was that the system was too costly, inefficient and ineffective.

In its first few months of office after assuming power in May 1997, the Labour Government published six consultation documents on the subject of youth crime, including a White Paper 'No More Excuses: A New Approach to Tackling Crime'. (HM Government, 1997). The title for this document provided an insight into the tone of the changes that the government wanted to make – no more excuses from young offenders, and no more excuses for practitioners (Open University/YJB). The results of these documents found their way into the government's major piece of legislation, the 1998 Crime and Disorder Act.

This act, described by Newburn as *a very significant piece of legislation* for New Labour (2003, page 210), was responsible for the establishment of the Youth Justice Board (YJB) and youth offending teams (YOT) which have statutory duties to prevent offending by children and young people. In addition to these structural changes, the Crime and Disorder Act also scrapped the caution (informal and formal) for young people and replaced it with the reprimand (for less serious offences) and final warning (for more serious offences – discussed in greater detail later in this chapter).

The role of the police

Youth justice policy under the Labour Government had been based on the theory and practice of prevention and rapid and early intervention with offenders (Waters, 2007, p 635). However, it is important to note that the police play a key role in youth justice. Waters (2007, p 635) notes that the 1998 government guidelines on youth justice, while emphasising prevention and the need for agency partnership, highlighted the role of the police in relation to administering swift justice, confronting offenders with the consequences of their behaviour, tackling the factors that put young people at risk of offending and contributing to local annual youth justice plans.

The 2003–06 National Policing Plan included the Home Office Public Service Agreement 5: this noted the need to reduce by 5 per cent the offending of young people (Home Office, 2002, p 42), and individual police forces have published their various youth strategies (see, e.g. Avon and Somerset Constabulary, 2003, cited in HMIC, 2004). Most young people enter the youth justice system when arrested by the police, and the role and behaviour of the latter are crucial (Audit Commission, 2004, p 14; Waters, 2007, p 635).

The Labour Government's Youth Crime Action Plan (2008) set out what it termed a *'triple track' approach of enforcement and punishment where behaviour is unacceptable, non-negotiable support and challenge where it is most needed, and better and earlier prevention* (HM Government, 2008, p 1). This document suggested that *reductions in youth crime will principally come about if we reduce the flow of young people entering the criminal justice system. Each year, around 100,000 young people aged 10–17 enter the criminal justice system for the first time. Our new goal is to reduce the rate by one fifth by 2020* (HM Government, 2008, p 14). The success of Labour policy with regard to young offenders would be measured against *five key, visible improvements for the public.*

1. *Swifter action taken against young people involved in crime and disorder.*

2. *Problems tackled before they spiral out of control, including parents taking more responsibility for their children.*

3. *Better support for young victims.*

4. *More sentences that people can see and have a greater say in, and that deal with the causes of offending.*

5. *Effective punishment backed up by support for young offenders to ensure public protection and effective resettlement.*

(HM Government, 2008, p 14).

In a speech in November 2010, Minister Crispin Blunt outlined the following as key areas of the government's approach to young offenders.

'Firstly, secure accommodation will remain the most appropriate place to deal with a small proportion of young offenders. And we must accept that there will be occasions when a remand to custody will also be appropriate for a young person. But I believe the use of custodial remand is currently too high and I am keen to see this addressed. Spending on youth remand could be better used to develop local solutions which would be more cost effective in the long term, and allow young people to be diverted away from a potentially unnecessary period in custody.

Secondly, I believe there is still not enough emphasis placed on the importance of young offenders paying back to society, and especially to victims, for the harm they have caused. Using restorative justice approaches is a crucial element of this. I fully support the principles of restorative justice in bringing together those who have a stake in a conflict to collectively resolve it; both as an alternative to the criminal justice system and as an addition to it. Thirdly, I am also clear that in order to make real progress in reducing reoffending and protecting the public, we must look to do more to address the factors that cause these individuals to offend, and go on offending' (Blunt, 2010).

These views were given concrete form in December 2010 when the coalition government produced a Green Paper 'Breaking the Cycle: Effective Punishment, Rehabilitation and Sentencing of Offenders' which indicated the direction that it intended to pursue with regard to criminal justice policy, including attempts to address offending by young people (Ministry of Justice, 2010).

Look at the youth justice policy outlined by New Labour in its 2008 Youth Crime Action Plan (available at www.justice.gov.uk/publications/docs/youth-crime-action-plan.pdf). Then, examine the current government's proposals outlined in its 'Breaking the Cycle' document (available at www.justice.gov.uk/consultations/docs/breaking-the-cycle.pdf). What are the similarities and differences between these two policy documents?

Notwithstanding the attempts by the current government to distance its approach on sentencing and criminal justice from that adopted by New Labour (and the preamble to the Government's Green Paper states that the criminal justice system is *so badly in need of reform* (Ministry of Justice, 2010)), the priorities identified in the Green Paper appear broadly to continue in the direction pursued by the previous Labour administration.

The specific measures discussed by the Green Paper in respect of preventing offending by young people are to encourage YOTs to use parenting orders where parents will not face up to their responsibilities, simplify out-of-court disposals and increase the use of restorative justice (Ministry of Justice, 2010, p 67). To help achieve these aims, the Green Paper will *allow police and prosecutors greater discretion in dealing with youth crime before it reaches court. We propose to end the current system of automatic escalation and instead put our trust in the professionals who are working with young people on the ground. The police, working in partnership with other local agencies, will have more freedom to determine the most appropriate response, depending on the severity of the offence and the circumstances of the young offender. This could involve reparation or interventions such as a referral to mental health provision to tackle offending behaviour* (Ministry of Justice, 2010, p 69).

With regard to the work of YOTs, the Green Paper says *Youth Offending Teams are the responsibility of local authorities, who have a statutory duty to prevent offending by young people. The arrangement works well and we do not propose to make fundamental changes to the model of Youth Offending Teams at this time* (Ministry of Justice, 2010, p 72). One notable proposed change in the Green Paper is the suggestion that local authorities should incur the costs if a young person enters custody; currently, these costs are borne centrally by the Ministry of Justice.

> *There has long been an argument that local agencies lack the incentive, and the opportunity, to develop effective alternatives to custody for young people …. We think there is more potential to test approaches that will incentivise and reward areas that are successful in intervening early to stop young people entering and escalating through the criminal justice system and in providing effective resettlement …. Specifically, we are proposing that local authorities should share both the financial risk of young people entering custody and the financial rewards if fewer young people require a custodial sentence.*
>
> (Ministry of Justice, 2010, p 73)

Multi-agency approaches and partnership working

The needs of young people have historically been catered for by a range of public agencies who have not always found it easy to work together effectively because of their different traditions, cultures and perspectives (Joyce, 2006). The 1998 Crime and Disorder Act sought to tackle this by introducing measures to enable a multi-agency or partnership approach towards preventing juvenile crime and dealing with juvenile offenders, primarily through the establishment of the YOT (Joyce, 2006).

Youth Justice Board

YJB was established by the 1998 Crime and Disorder Act. Currently, the YJB is the organisation that oversees the youth justice system in England and Wales (although in October 2010, as part of the government's 'reform of public bodies', it was announced that the YJB would be abolished and its functions absorbed within the Ministry of Justice). Its board members are appointed by the secretary of state for justice. On its website, the YJB identifies its objectives as being:

- to advise the Secretary of State on the operation of, and standards for, the youth justice system;

- to monitor the performance of the youth justice system;

- to purchase places for, and place, children and young people remanded or sentenced to custody;

- to identify and promote effective practice;

- to make grants to local authorities and other bodies to support the development of effective practice;

- to commission research and publish information.

(YJB website)

Youth offending teams

YOTs were also established under the 1998 Crime and Disorder Act, their function being the supervision of all young people entering the youth justice system. They became operational nationally in 2000, with the YJB being tasked to monitor their performance.

Their establishment was primarily in response to the earlier conclusions by the Audit Commission (contained in the 1996 report 'Misspent Youth') that existing youth justice interventions were expensive and ineffective. *A key rationale for establishing YOTs was to ensure that YOT officers were drawn from the main agencies that were, de facto, involved in managing young offenders prior to 2000, in order to avoid duplication, inconsistencies and variation in priorities* (Ellis and Boden, nd, p 1, citing Home Office, 1997).

New Labour's belief in partnership working was reflected in the membership of the YOT. The 1998 Crime and Disorder Act introduced a statutory requirement that the following services had to be represented in YOTs: social services, police, the probation service, education/schools and the health service. Initially, membership of the YOT was dominated by social services, who contributed 55 per cent to the YOTs, followed by the police (13 per cent), probation (10 per cent),

Local Authority Chief Executives (9 per cent), education (7 per cent) and health (6 per cent) (Renshaw and Powell, 2001, quoted in Newburn, 2003).

The Crime and Disorder Act also placed a statutory duty on local authorities to formulate and implement annual youth justice plans. These stipulated how youth justice services were to be provided and funded locally, how YOTs were to oper- ate and be funded locally and the functions they would carry out. In producing these, the local authorities had to consult with the senior officers of the major agencies (police, probation and health) that made up the YOTs (Newburn, 2003, page 211). These reports in turn had to be published and submitted to the YJB in recognition of its role as monitor of local provision and advisor to the home secretary.

Effectiveness of YOTs

Studies of the early implementation of YOTs *tended to paint a generally confusing and problematic picture* (Ellis and Boden, nd, p 3), with assertions about conflicts between the various agencies (and 'cultural hangovers' from previous youth justice practice (Bailey and Williams, 2000, and Holdaway, Davidson, Dignan, Hammersley, Hine and Mash, 2001, both cited in Ellis and Boden, nd, p 3), although it has been suggested that some of the early criticisms of YOTs stemmed in part from the commentators' (notably Goldson, Pitt and Muncie) concerns about the philosophi- cal and ideological direction of policy under New Labour, and the directing role played by the YJB (Ellis and Boden, nd). Subsequent research (notably Ellis and Boden, nd, developing Burnett and Appleton's, 2004, work) suggests that *those from different professional backgrounds have very similar views on what their role is in supervising young offenders, and that this role is primarily about care rather than control/coerced treatment … and that all YOT workers, irrespective of parent agency, are clearly towards the welfare end of the welfare-justice continuum* (Ellis and Boden, nd, p 11).

What do the YOTs do?

There is a YOT in every local authority in England and Wales. They are made up of representatives from the police, probation service, social services, health, educa- tion, drugs and alcohol misuse and housing officers. Each YOT is managed by a YOT manager who is responsible for co-ordinating the work of the youth justice services. The two primary functions of the YOTs are to co-ordinate the provision of youth justice services for all those in the local authority's area who need them and to carry out such functions as are assigned to the team in the youth justice plan formulated by the local authority (Newburn, 2003, p 211).

Because the YOT incorporates representatives from a wide range of services, it can respond to the needs of young offenders in a comprehensive way. The YOT identifies the needs of each young offender by assessing them with a national assessment. It identifies the specific problems that make the young person offend and measures the risk they pose to others. This enables the YOT to identify suitable programmes to address the needs of the young person with the intention of preventing further offending (YJB website).

Assessment

YOTs use a range of assessments to identify the needs of young people, the risk they present to themselves and others and the likelihood of them offending or reoffending.

REFLECTIVE TASK

In Chapter 2, you read about the various factors that impact the likelihood of offending by young people. Bearing these in mind, what are the factors that you anticipate the YOTs would consider when making an assessment of the risks presented by young people and the likelihood of them (re)offending?

The assessments used by YOTs require them to speak to the young person, their parents and other services that have worked with them or their family, and gather information about their:

- criminal history (if they have already offended);
- education;
- health;
- family;
- environment;
- attitudes.

YOTs use the information from these assessments to create programmes of activities for the young person that address their needs and aim to reduce the likelihood of offending, with the assessments being reviewed and updated in the light of changes in the young person's circumstances. There are two forms of assessment used by the YOTs: Asset and Onset.

Asset

For young people who have offended, the YOT uses an assessment called Asset, which has to be completed with young people (a) subject to a final warning or (b) due to be sentenced to a custodial or community order. The YOT uses the information from the assessment to:

- make a recommendation to the court on a suitable sentence;
- identify the activities that the young person will be required to complete as part of their sentence;

- identify whether work needs to be done with their parents/carers;
- identify how to protect the public.

In turn, if a young person is sentenced or remanded to custody, the information gathered by Asset will be used by the YOT to assess whether the young person is vulnerable. The information will then be used by the YJB to decide the type of custodial establishment the young person should be placed in (YJB website, Youth Justice Board, 2006, 2008).

Onset

For young people who have been identified as being *at risk of offending*, the YOT uses an assessment called Onset. Onset is used to identify whether a young person would benefit from participating in a prevention programme and to identify their needs and how best these needs should be addressed so as to reduce the likelihood of them subsequently going on to offend. Onset helps to identify risk factors to be reduced and protective factors to be enhanced. It also provides information which might be helpful in selecting appropriate interventions for those identified as needing early intervention. When collated, the information on Onset can be used for monitoring and targeting specific sub-groups where applicable, or providing progress data to steering groups (YJB website – www.yjb.gov.uk/en-gb/practitioners/Assessment/Onset.htm).

The criminal justice system and young people

Youth court

When a young person is charged with an offence, they will typically appear before the youth court. If the case cannot be dealt with immediately, the court will make a decision as to whether the young person will be bailed or remanded to custody.

Adult magistrates' courts only try and sentence people for offences where the maximum penalty is six months in prison. They deal mainly with cases involving people over the age of 18 and will only deal with young people if they are being tried with an adult. The youth court is a section of the magistrates' court (it may even be located in the same building) and deals with almost all cases involving young people under the age of 18. Those serving the youth court (youth panel magistrates and district judges) have the power to give a range of community sentences.

Youth courts tend to be less formal than magistrates' courts, are more open and engage more with the young person appearing in court and their family. Members of the public are not allowed in, although the victim(s) of the crime may attend court hearings should they wish, but they must have made a request to the court to do so. Victims also have the opportunity to have an input into the sentencing process via the YOT (YJB website).

If a young person pleads not guilty, a date will be set for the trial when the magistrates will hear all the evidence and decide whether or not the young person is guilty. If the decision is guilty, they will then decide on the most appropriate sentence. If the case is very serious, the youth court will send the case to the Crown Court for trial and/or sentence (YJB website: www.yjb.gov.uk/en-gb/yjs/Courts/).

Prevention of youth crime

One of the best and most cost-effective ways to reduce youth crime is to prevent young people from getting into trouble in the first place by dealing with the problems that make it more likely they will commit crime or anti-social behaviour. An Audit Commission report in 2004 estimated that early intervention to prevent young people offending could save public services more than £80 million a year. Problems that may lead to a young person's troublesome behaviour include a lack of education, poor family relationships, having family members or peers who have offended and misuse of substances (discussed in more detail in Chapter 2). A number of programmes aiming to deal with risk factors, engage young people's interests and increase their knowledge have been introduced.

Intensive Supervision and Surveillance Programme

The Intensive Supervision and Surveillance Programme (ISSP) can be a condition of bail, or a Youth Rehabilitation Order (YRO, discussed in more detail below). The YJB website describes ISSP as a *mixture of punishment and positive opportunities, available 365 days a year, providing the courts with a robust alternative to custody*, which should always contain the following core elements.

- Education, training or employment.

- Restorative justice.

- Offending behaviour.

- Family support.

- Interpersonal skills.

Overall, the ISSP is designed to:

- ensure that the young person makes recompense for his/her offences;

- address the underlying causes of the offending;

- put in place structures that will allow the young person to avoid offending in the future;

- manage the risks posed by the young person to the community;

- stabilise what is often a very chaotic lifestyle;

- reintegrate the young person into the community, particularly through activities that can be continued when supervision by the YOT has ended;

- help the young person lead an independent life free of offending.
  (YJB website at www.yjb.gov.uk/en-gb/yjs/SentencesOrdersandAgreements/ISS/)

An early evaluation of ISSP (Little et al., 2004) found that while the intervention did not have an impact on reconviction rates (comparing those randomly allocated to ISSP with two control groups), there was a 30 per cent to 50 per cent reduction in the amount of crime committed by ISSP participants.

Youth Inclusion Programme

Youth Inclusion Programmes (YIPs) were established in 2000 and are *tailor-made programmes for 8 to 17-year-olds, who are identified as being at high risk of involvement in offending or anti-social behaviour* (YJB website). YIPs are also open to other young people in the local area. Young people on the YIP are identified through a number of different agencies including YOTs, police, social services, local education authorities or schools and other local agencies (YJB website). A more detailed account of the work of YIPs is provided in Chapter 6.

Youth Inclusion and Support Panels

Youth Inclusion and Support Panels (YISPs) aim to prevent anti-social behaviour and offending by 8- to 13-year-olds who are considered to be at *high risk of offending*. They have been designed to help the YJB meet its target of putting in place, in each YOT in England and Wales, programmes that will identify and reduce the likelihood of young people committing offences.

Panels are made up of a number of representatives from different agencies (e.g. the police, schools and health and social services). The main emphasis of the panel's work is to ensure that children and their families, at the earliest possible opportunity, can access mainstream public services (YJB website).

Diversion

According to Newburn and Souhami (2005), *like so many terms in criminology and criminal justice, 'diversion' defies easy definition*, but at its most basic aims to minimise the extent of contact between young offenders and the criminal justice system so as to reduce the stigmatising effects of involvement with the criminal justice system and preventing the reoffending that follows from the establishment of delinquent identities (in Tilley (ed), 2005, p 355). This approach builds on the recognition (e.g. in the 1980 White Paper) that juvenile offenders who could be diverted away from the criminal justice system at an early stage in their offending were less likely to reoffend than those who became involved in judicial proceedings (Newburn, 2003, p 198).

REFLECTIVE TASK

Think about the reasons why diverting young people away from the criminal just-ice system might be an effective way of reducing youth offending. What forms might this diversion take?

Diversion may cover a range of different aspects of the criminal justice system and criminal careers: *diversion from custody* (via the use of activities and programmes aimed at reducing the extent of imprisonment of young offenders), *diversion from the courts* (via the formal processing of young offenders in the criminal justice system) and *diversion from crime* (via attempts to decrease the extent of juvenile offending, shorten the length of juvenile criminal careers or even to prevent the onset of a criminal career altogether) (Newburn and Souhami, 2005).

One of the central agencies in attempts to increase diversion has been the police, particularly through their increased use of cautioning (an example of diversion away from the courts). This stems from the recognition (covered in more detail in Chapter 6) that the police have a great deal of discretion in dealing with offenders, particularly young offenders. Throughout the 1970s, 1980s and 1990s, there were a succession of Home Office Circulars encouraging the police to use their powers to caution (the 1990 circular, for example, explicitly countenancing offenders being cautioned more than once, *provided the nature and circumstances of the most recent offence warrant it* (Newburn, 2003, p 198)), although there remained great variation in the use of cautions by police forces.

Community sentences

When young people first get into trouble, behave anti-socially or commit minor offences, they can usually be dealt with by the police and local authority outside the court system, using a variety of orders and agreements. This is to stop young people getting sucked into the youth justice system too early, while still offering them the help and support they need to stop offending.

Reprimands and final warnings

If an offender is aged under 18 and found guilty of a minor crime, they may receive a reprimand or a warning from the police.

A reprimand is a formal verbal warning given by a police officer to a young person who admits they are guilty of a minor first offence. Sometimes, the young person can be referred to the YOT to take part in a voluntary programme to help them address their offending behaviour (YJB website).

A final warning is a formal verbal warning given by a police officer to a young person who admits their guilt for a first or second offence. Unlike a reprimand, however, the young person is also assessed to determine the causes of their offending behaviour, and a programme of activities is identified to address them (YJB website).

The magistrate or a judge will consider a number of things before deciding what punishment the young person will receive, including:

- whether they have been reprimanded or warned before;
- how serious the offence was;
- the number of offences committed.

On receipt of a final warning, the offender is likely to be contacted by their local YOT to ascertain the reasons why the young person is offending and develop an action plan to prevent it recurring. Under-18s who have received a reprimand or warning before are likely to be given a more serious punishment, like a YRO (Direct Gov website – community sentences).

Youth Rehabilitation Orders

YROs were introduced in 2009 and are the generic community sentence for children and young people who offend, replacing nine existing sentences (including curfew orders, attendance centre orders, drug treatment and testing orders and supervision orders), combining 18 requirements into one generic sentence. According to the YJB website, *having 18 requirements within one Order will simplify sentencing, providing clarity and coherence while improving the flexibility of interventions* while allowing *plenty of opportunity for reparation to be included, giving scope for victims' needs to be addressed* (YJB website at www.yjb.gov.uk/en-gb/yjs/SentencesOrdersandAgreements/YRO/).

When a court gives a YRO, it decides the most appropriate 'requirements' to attach to it, depending on the details of the case. Requirements that those found guilty may be asked to complete include:

- treatment for mental health and drug misuse;
- supervision;
- curfew;
- unpaid work;
- electronic monitoring;
- repairing any damage that they may have caused.

Young offenders may get a YRO if:

- it is their first offence and they have pleaded not guilty;
- it is their second or third offence.

(Direct Gov website – community sentences)

Anti-social behaviour measures

There are a range of measures available to the police and other agencies to deal with anti-social behaviour by young people and adults. You read about a number of these (notably Anti-Social Behaviour Orders and Acceptable Behaviour Contracts) in the previous chapter. However, there are a number of other sanctions that are available to the police and other agencies to tackle anti-social behaviour by young people (and their parents).

Parenting orders

A Parenting Order is a court order which usually means a parent or carer must attend parenting classes (sometimes called parenting programmes/interventions). Parents may also be ordered to meet other conditions, like making sure their child stays at home at certain times, or attend meetings with their child's teachers. These can last for up to three months and are intended to help improve the child's behaviour.

They can be given when a pupil has been excluded from school for serious bad behaviour, either permanently or for the second time in 12 months. They can also be applied for as a result of persistent truanting, when a child or young person has displayed (or is at risk of displaying) anti-social or criminal behaviour and when parenting is considered a factor in the child's behaviour (Direct Gov website).

Restorative justice

There can be little doubt that there was a concerted effort by New Labour to make both victims' views and reparation more central aspects of youth just-ice than had previously been the case (Newburn, 2003, page 217). There was much of the 1998 Crime and Disorder Act that was based on ideas influenced by restorative justice (notably the reformed cautioning system, action plan orders and reparation orders that all sought to promote the idea of reparation, and seek the victim's views), although the extent of the change brought in by the 1998 act (sometimes depicted as a restorative justice revolution) has been overstated (Newburn, 2003).

The action plan order was designed to be the first option for young offenders whose offending was serious enough to warrant a community sentence. It was described (in the 'No More Excuses' document) as a *short intensive programme of community intervention combining punishment, rehabilitation, and reparation to change offending behaviour and prevent further crime* (Home Office, 1997, cited in Newburn, 2003, p 217).

The reparation order is a community order supervised by a member of the YOT which aims to prevent further offending by helping the offender to understand the effects of crime on the victim and to make amends. Typically, it would involve the offender attending sessions to understand about the effect their crime may have had on the victim(s) and community, writing a letter to apologise and meeting the victim (if the victim so wishes) so that the offender can apologise in person and carry out some practical work for the victim or the for the community. If the offender does not cooperate with the reparation order, he or she will be returned to court. The court may:

- order the offender to complete the order;

- fine the offender up to £1,000;

- discharge the order and sentence the offender in a different way for the original offence.

(North Somerset Council Youth Offending Team, 2002).

Attempts to expand the use of restorative justice were contained in the Labour Government's 2009 assessment of the impact of the previous year's 'Action Plan for Youth Crime' (HM Government, 2009), and have continued in the coalition government's consultation Green Paper 'Breaking the Cycle: Effective Punishment, Rehabilitation and Sentencing of Offenders' (Ministry of Justice, 2010).

C H A P T E R   S U M M A R Y

Youth justice practice is an arena where the police play a varied and important role – whether it be in diverting young offenders, or those deemed at risk of offending, away from the criminal justice system or the courts via the use of reprimands or final warnings, or in the supervision of young offenders (via their involvement in YOTs or YISPs). The precise direction of the current government's policy in regard to young offenders (as so much else in the policing and community safety arena) is currently under review, but it is certain that the police will continue to play a central part. Chapter 6 will look in greater detail at their engagement with young people in a more informal role.

FURTHER READING

The most accurate picture of current proposals for reform of the criminal justice system, including those relating to young offenders, is to be found in the government's consultation document 'Breaking the Cycle', and the various responses to this document. This can be found at the consultation site on the Ministry of Justice website: www.justice.gov.uk/consultations/breaking-cycle-071210.htm.

Good general accounts of the development of youth justice services can be found in Tim Newburn's *Crime and Criminal Justice Policy* (2nd edition, 2003), chapter 8, 'Youth Crime and Youth Justice' and Peter Joyce's 2006 *Criminal Justice; An Introduction to Crime and the Criminal Justice System*, chapter 9 'Juvenile Crime and the State's Response'.

YJB website section on youth justice services contains some very useful information about what the YJB does, the role of the YOTs and the various disposals available for young people. Currently, this is available at www.yjb.gov.uk/en-gb/yjs/.

REFERENCES

Audit Commission (1996) *Misspent Youth*. London: Audit Commission.

Audit Commission (2004) *Youth Justice 2004: A Review of the Reformed Youth Justice System*. London: Audit Commission.

Blunt, C (2010) 'Vision for Youth Justice' speech, available at Ministry of Justice website: www.justice.gov.uk/news/sp241110.htm (accessed 18 March 2011).

Burnett, R and Appleton, C (2004) Joined-up Services to Tackle Youth Crime. *British Journal of Criminology*, 44(1): 34–54.

Campbell, B (1993) *Goliath – Britain's Dangerous Places*. London: Methuen.

Direct Gov Website. Parenting orders, ASBOs and other behaviour orders at www.direct.gov.uk/en/Parents/CrimeAndYoungOffenders/DG_071214 (accessed 18 March 2011).

Ellis, T and Boden, I (nd) *Is There a Unifying Professional Culture in Youth Offending Teams? A Research Note*. Available online at www.britsoccrim.org/volume7/006.pdf (accessed 18 March 2011).

HM Government (1997) *No More Excuses; A New Approach Towards Tackling Youth Crime in England and Wales*. Available online at webarchive.nationalarchives.gov.uk/+/ www.homeoffice.gov.uk/documents/jou-no-more-excuses?view=Html.

HM Government (2008) *Youth Crime Action Plan 2008*.

HM Government (2009) *Youth Crime Action Plan: One Year On*. Available online at webarchive.nationalarchives.gov.uk/20100405140447/ www.homeoffice.gov.uk/documents/youth-crime-action-plan/one-year-on-survey2835.pdf?view=Binary (accessed 22 March 2011).

HMIC (2004) *Baseline Assessment (Revised) of Avon and Somerset Constabulary*. Available online at www.hmic.gov.uk/SiteCollectionDocuments/Avon%20and%20Somerset/BLA_AVS_20040930.pdf (accessed 19 May 2011).

Home Office (2002) *National Policing Plan 2003–06*. London: Home Office.

Hughes, G, McLaughlin, E and Muncie, J (2002) *Crime Prevention and Community Safety: New Directions*. London: Sage.

Joyce, P (2006) *Criminal Justice: An Introduction to Crime and the Criminal Justice System*. Cullompton, Devon: Willan Publishing.

Little, M, Kogan, J, Bullock, R and van der Laan, P (2004) ISSP: An experiment in multi-systemic responses to persistent young offenders. *British Journal of Criminology*, **44**: 225–40.

Ministry of Justice (2010) *Breaking the Cycle: Effective Punishment, Rehabilitation and Sentencing of Offenders*. London: Ministry of Justice.

Newburn, T (2002) Young People, Crime and Youth Justice in Maguire M, Morgan R and Reiner R (eds) *The Oxford Handbook of Criminology*. Oxford: Oxford University Press.

Newburn, T (2003) *Crime and Criminal Justice Policy*, 2nd edition. Longman Criminology Series. Harlow: Longman.

Newburn, T and Souhami, A (2005) Youth Diversion in Tilley, N (ed) *Handbook of Crime Prevention.* Cullompton, Devon: Willan Publishing.

North Somerset Council Youth Offending Team (2002) *What is a Reparation Order?* Available online at www.n-somerset.gov.uk/NR/rdonlyres/1CC1AA59–1346–4D98–9B6E-A146B2E0010C/0/leaflet_200602_ReparationOrderMay02.pdf (accessed 27 March 2011).

Open University/YJB *A Brief History of the Youth Justice System.* labspace.open.ac.uk/file.php/5193/YJ_k523_1/sco.htm#

Pratt, J (1989) Corporatism: The Third Model of Juvenile Justice, *British Journal of Criminology*, 29: 236–54.

Waters, I (2007) The policing of young offenders. *British Journal of Criminology*, **47**: 635–54.

Youth Justice Board (2006). *The Common Assessment Framework, Asset and Onset; Guidance for Youth Justice Practitioners.* London: YJB for England and Wales.

Youth Justice Board (2008). *Key Elements of Effective Practice; Assessment, Planning Interventions and Supervision.* London: YJB for England and Wales.

USEFUL WEBSITES

www.direct.gov.uk/en/Parents/CrimeAndYoungOffenders/DG_071214 (Direct Gov website – Parenting orders, ASBOs and other behaviour orders).

www.homeoffice.gov.uk/police/powers/ (Home Office website on police powers).

labspace.open.ac.uk/file.php/5193/YJ_k523_1/sco.htm# (Open University/YJB 'A Brief History of the Youth Justice System').

www.yjb.gov.uk/en-gb/ (YJB website).

www.yjb.gov.uk/timeline/ (Ten years of Youth Justice Reform (timeline of reforms between 1998 – 2008) available from the YJB website).

6 Engaging with young people

Introduction

This chapter considers the engagement process between the police and young people prior to any formal involvement with the criminal justice system. In particular, the chapter considers the relationship between the police and crime prevention schemes, evaluating the utility of such schemes in the broader context of social crime prevention. It also considers the way in which the police interact with young people and discusses the use of discretion along with the problems of stereotyping young people before engagement.

Young people as negative identities

We have seen in a separate chapter how young people can be portrayed through the media and how this affects others' perception of them. This can be particularly strong. For example, if you were to say anti-social behaviour, the chances are that most people would immediately associate young people with the term, when clearly any person can commit anti-social behaviour.

Identity

When we think about society and life in general, we realise that it is not always harmonious. Relationships between people are not necessarily equal or mutually beneficial but can involve an imbalance of power and a lopsided, damaging connection. For example, in the case of a police officer in uniform interacting with a group of young people on the street, the power and the discretion with which to use the power lays with the police officer because of his/her legal sanctions. The relationships that exist between individuals and groups can often be described in terms of identity.

During the 1980s, Raban (1991) went to New York and noticed the negative way in which other people talked about street people (those who lived on the streets or suffered from alcoholism, etc.). Despite the fact that each of these people had separate identities, they were put together in one large identity – *the street people*. Raban decided to experiment with his ideas and set out to act like a member of the so-called street people. Read the following extract from Raban's work.

> *On West 22nd at Broadway I found a vacant fire hydrant, and settled on it, as in an armchair, like the street people did, to watch the crowd file past. Everyone moved with the same stiff clockwork action; everyone wore the same hard-boiled look on their face. As they approached my fire hydrant, they accelerated slightly from the waist down, locked their eyes into the horizontal position, and swept by, giving me an exaggeratedly wide berth. I tried making eye contact, and managed to catch a few pairs of pupils' off-guard: they swerved away in their sockets, as quick as fish. It was interesting to feel oneself being willed into non-existence by total strangers. I'd never felt the force of such frank contempt – and all because I was sitting on a fire hydrant.*
> (Raban, 1991, pp 79–80)

This example illustrates how street identities can sometimes be performed by others, but it reminds us of how we are seen by others. The poor and unemployed people on the street discussed above were perceived as different from the kind of group who all knew each other and had shared beliefs, etc. Street people are ascribed a label which relates to their negative collective identity which once given sticks to a person and it is difficult to escape. They were allocated a negative identity to 'them', 'not us'. This experiment highlights a common pattern in the relational identities of groups. On one side of the relationship is a group of 'them' with a detailed negative identity. On the other side are 'us' with a vaguely positive 'normal' identity which is not really described but is sometimes called the unmarked identity. This way of dividing up people is referred to as 'othering'. Before moving on, try the following exercise.

PRACTICAL TASK

Write down on a piece of paper groups of people that you think you might consider as 'others' and ascribe to them a detailed negative identity. What is there in reality that supports your view? Upon reflection, is this view a correct one?

'Othering' can explain why we see and react to people as we do. It may be the case that young people in general are seen by the police as not being like 'us' and do not share 'our' values and norms. For example, they may dress differently, hang around street corners and listen to loud music which irritates people. They are therefore 'others', not like 'us', and are to be feared, their views discredited and they are seen as an enduring scapegoat for the collective ills in society. This belief in negative identities can be a barrier to the way in which police interact with young people in their normal day-to-day activities. A poor understanding of how we identify others can lead to pre-conceived ideas concerning individuals and groups and in the case of the police, can influence their manner and attitudes when exercising their discretion when dealing with young people.

Police discretion and young people

Discretion is an established legal activity essential for police officers in their choice as to whether to exercise their powers or not. It is the impact of a police officer's powers on an individual or a community that makes the issue of 'discretion' so far-reaching.

REFLECTIVE TASK

Write down what discretion means to you. Once you have done this, compare it with the definition below.

One definition suggests that discretion is:

- *freedom of judgement and action;*

- *the authority to decide and choose;*

- *selecting the best course of action, having recognised and considered all of the alternatives.*

(Rogers, 2008, p 100)

It may be the case that certain sections of society, for example, young people, suffer disproportionately as a result of how police officers use their powers of discretion. The problem, however, is not just with the definition of 'discretion', which is a subjective one, but an individual officer's interpretation of 'police powers' and their discretionary use. In America, for example, unethical use of discretion was identified as a major drive in growing unlawful activity within policing during the 1960s. For example, the black civil rights movement argued that black people were being disproportionately subject to the police use of discretion when exercising their powers. In the United Kingdom, things have been viewed differently. It is a long established fact of policing that police officers exercise considerable discretion in the way they carry out their duties, as Reiner (2000) identifies:

> All police forces have been characterised by the discretion exercised by the
> lower ranks in the organisation, a discretion facilitated above all by the basic
> nature of police work as dispersed surveillance.
>
> (Reiner, 2000, p 7)

Indeed, lawful and ethical discretion may be claimed to be one of the most powerful weapons in a police officer's armoury and is essential if the police are to police by consent. However, young people, in general, and black youths, in particular, appear to be disproportionately affected by police use of discretion, and historically this has been cited as one of the main causes of the breakdown of relationships between minority ethnic youth communities and the police (Allen et al., 2006). The use of discretion by the police is the interpretation of terms such as 'reasonable suspicion' and the powers to exercise detention for search and arrest by officers in their everyday duties.

Clearly, the application of discretion by the police when dealing with young people either on the street or elsewhere can be influenced by negative identity perceptions as discussed above. For example, Brown (1997) suggests that in terms of victimisation of youth, adults in general and the police in particular do not take it seriously, leading to young people developing their own strategies for coping with crime, some of which may involve them in offending, such as carrying weapons for protection, while others 'reinforce' their invisibility, by, for example, not coming forward as witnesses. The whole cycle of indifference both reinforces young people's vulnerability and makes it more likely that they will be identified as 'problematic' and 'offenders' by the police.

Reasons for engagement

Before considering the major type of approach that underlines why the police should become involved with, and engage with, young people, it is best perhaps to understand the types of levels of intervention with young people that exist. In the main, these are considered useful in the prevention of crime and disorder issues as they are aimed at specifically frustrating future or present instances of crime and disorder. Commonly referred to as the 'Three Levels of Intervention,' this approach drew its inspiration from medicine and the natural sciences, and was first discussed and considered in the mid-1970s by Brantingham and Faust (1976).

Three levels of intervention

Level 1 — Primary level

Within this approach, energies are directed towards preventing the onset of criminality, and known risk factors associated with childhood anti-social behaviour have been identified. These include poverty and poor housing, poor parenting, association with delinquent peers and poor school attendance. These approaches tend to focus on the general population of potential offenders. Children who are exposed to multiple risks are more likely to become serious or persistent offenders. This approach is visible in the school curriculum which contains elements such as good citizenship.

Level 2 — Secondary level

This approach focuses on those particularly at risk of offending or victimisation. These individuals or groups have been identified because of some predispositional factors. This could be their age group, where they live, their lifestyle, their socio-economic circumstances or some other predictor of risk. As a consequence, the target audience is deemed to be more prone to criminality and therefore worthy of attention. An example of this type of approach can be seen in school education initiatives about the use of illegal drugs and other substances.

Level 3 — Tertiary level

This level attempts to deal with those already convicted or victimised, through crime prevention initiatives such as 'Homesafe' schemes which target harden burglary victims' homes against repeat offences, through to restorative justice. Restorative justice techniques aim to bring together offender and victim in order to encourage the offender to make restoration of loss, either in the material or emotional sense, to the victim.

This approach revolves around the nature of the relationship between the intended audience and the form of prevention on offer. So primary prevention is aimed at the general population with no pre-conceived assumptions about their propensity to commit crime and disorder. Secondary prevention, on the other hand, assumes the audience is at risk in some way or other, while tertiary prevention is focused on reducing the criminality of people who already assumed to be criminals and also preventing victims of crime becoming repeat victims.

This approach is illustrated in Figure 6.1.

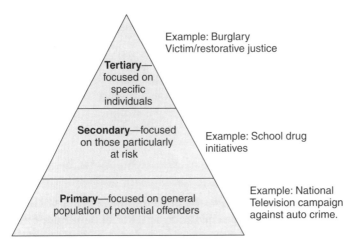

Figure 6.1 Three levels of crime and disorder reduction

PRACTICAL TASK

Having explained the three levels of intervention, attempt the following exercise. Alongside the entry in the left-hand column, place in the right-hand column what you think is the level of intervention.

Initiative	Level of intervention
Radio programme informing people not to carry suspicious packages through customs for people.	
Driving proficiency course for those caught speeding in their vehicles.	
Youth club talk by the police on the use of illegal drugs.	

The first initiative is clearly a primary intervention aimed at the general public, while the third initiative fits the definition of the tertiary level of intervention. The youth club talk example is a secondary level of intervention aimed at those who may be considered at risk.

Having discussed the differing levels of intervention available to police practitioner when attempting to influence communities and young people in terms of crime and disorder reduction, he or she should also be aware of the two distinctive types of crime prevention currently underpinning policies and strategies in this country.

Types of crime prevention measures

The main distinction in types of crime prevention measures is that of 'social' and 'situational' approaches, although it must be acknowledged at the outset that not all crime and disorder prevention initiatives fit neatly into these two main approaches, and that there are occasions when both styles are in operation together. Situational techniques, such as the use of Mosquito sound devices to move young people away from certain areas, have been discussed elsewhere in this book. This chapter will concentrate on a different approach, that of 'social' crime prevention.

Social crime prevention method

This approach of preventing or reducing crime and disorder is carried out by targeting anti-social behaviour and those at risk, as well as known offenders. It also includes programmes aimed at improving the opportunities of 'at risk' groups through community involvement. This approach tends to focus on the development of schemes such as youth clubs and activity-based projects to deter potential or actual offenders from future offending. Bright (1991) believes this approach also has an impact on agencies attempting this approach.

Point to note: social crime prevention

It aims to strengthen social agencies and community institutions in order to influence those groups that are most at risk of offending (Bright, 1991, p 64).

While other types of crime prevention may reduce crime and disorder which occurs as a result of situational factors, for example, the nature of the physical environment, they may not be effective against types of crime such as ongoing domestic violence and homicides which occur as a result of personal and/or social factors. Measures to address situational factors can reduce the opportunities to commit such crimes and may improve perceptions of safety in the community but are unlikely to stop those who are strongly motivated to commit crime.

The best way to prevent repeat offenders from committing crimes is to stop them becoming criminals in the first place. The approach discussed in this section – social crime prevention – aims for this. It is based on an understanding that there are personal and social factors which make it more likely that someone will commit crimes (see 'Point to note'), and by addressing these, an individual will more likely be turned away from criminality.

PRACTICAL TASK

Before reading on, try the following exercise (you may find it useful to refer back to Chapter 2 for some help). Write down on a piece of paper what factors you think make it more likely that a person will commit crime or a deviant act. Having done so, compare them to the list below.

Factors that may make it more likely someone will commit crimes are the following.

- Schooling.

- Income and employment.

- Alcohol and other drug use.

- Peer relations.

- Moral beliefs and other cultural influences.

(Bright, 1991)

Being aware and understanding that young people may commit crime and engage in anti-social activity because of wider social factors is an important move away from seeing young people as a problem that can be dealt with by using a purely 'enforcement' style of policing. This idea supports the wider concept of creating communities that are resistant to criminal and anti-social acts.

Creating Crime-Resistant Communities

Before discussing this concept, consider the following exercise.

REFLECTIVE TASK

Why do you think it is important for the police to work with others in creating crime-resistant communities? Compare your thoughts with the following section.

A neighbourhood which has strong social bonds, where people take pride in their street and 'own' their public places, where the needs of all groups in the community are met and where people regard the area as an attractive and safe place to live and work, is likely to have a low crime rate (Wedlock, 2006). These neighbourhoods have a cohesion or organisation and solidity that mean they pull together and are able to resist crime and disorder. The following case study summarises some of the ideas that support the idea of community cohesion.

COMMUNITY COHESION

The following may be considered useful in creating neighbourhoods that have strong bonds.

Youth clubs, football clubs, junior theatrical societies, use of community centres for all sorts of activities, etc. In fact, any neighbourhood project which gets people to

---

meet each other, to cooperate or work together or to play together will encourage social bonding.

A good example of this is the playgroup. Throughout the country, young parents meet once or twice a week for their pre-school children to play together. That is the main purpose. However, the effect is to encourage friendships between parents, set up informal babysitting networks, give children peer groups and friends before they start formal schooling and transfer skills and information from experienced parents to new parents. Social bonds that begin in these meetings very often last for a person's life.

Police practitioners should be aware of how important cohesive communities are and should encourage and even assist in this process.

In short, the rationale for this approach is as follows.

- Community is critical for identifying and dealing with problems.
- Community is mostly understood in geographical terms, comprising those who live or work in a particular area.
- Agencies are expected to become more sensitive and responsive to the wishes of the community.
- Community members are expected to play a large part in the governance of their local areas.
- Communities that are 'involved' are less likely to face serious problems than communities that are uninvolved and mistrustful of each other.

Youth engagement events are a vital part of this process, and several examples are now discussed and considered.

A good example of communities working to create cohesiveness can be seen in the following case study, which uses an example from Australia.

CASE STUDY

The objective of the Good Neighbourhood Program (GNP) was to prevent and reduce crime through social and community development. The principle behind this approach is that the more social networks operate in a community and the denser and widespread these networks are the less likely residents are to tolerate anti-social behaviour and criminal behaviour or to engage in such behaviour.

The GNP was launched in 1988 by the Victorian State Government, and provided funding to councils to set up local crime prevention committees. The statewide framework for the GNP identified a number of priority areas.

- *Activities for young people at risk.*

- *Education, training and employment.*

- *Safety and security in the community.*

- *Drug and alcohol abuse.*

- *Minimising re-offending behaviour.*

- *Police-community relations.*

The integrated development of social, recreational and work-related skills was encouraged. Projects also encouraged contacts between people of different ages, genders and backgrounds. All projects were run within local government areas. The local council's role was to play a leadership and developmental function by managing and being accountable for the resources allocated to the projects, establishing and supporting the local GNP committee, providing opportunities for people/organisations to register interest and participate in GNP activities, ensuring local networks, organisations and people were made aware of the GNP, endorsing local GNP committee recommendations and contributing to the resourcing of projects.

(Rogers, 2006)

The neighbourhood was the focal point of the GNP, which sought to encourage development and cohesion at this level. Young people were a particular focus, with their skills being used wherever possible (with pay where this was available). The successful local committees had strong council involvement and enthusiastic co-ordinators, support from local councillors and mayors and the involvement of local police. Further, youth service co-ordinators and a clear focus on crime prevention were characteristics of this successful local programme.

One of the most famous social intervention programmes for children and young people was the early intervention programme called the Perry Pre-School Programme, which was introduced in the United States between 1962 and 1967. Based on the belief that early intervention programmes can impact upon the quality of life, this programme was based on the belief that this kind of social intervention could help children in poverty make a better start in life.

Children aged between 3 and 4 years were randomly selected and assigned to two groups: one group received an active learning programme involving different educational inputs from different agencies and parental support and the other group did not receive this assistance. At the age of 40, the groups were revisited, and it was found that the group receiving the pre-school input had half the number of arrests of the other group, higher educational levels and higher levels of home ownership.

The apparent effects of this type of intervention and engagement on adult criminality was only one element in a much wider range of benefits, but clearly this programme highlights the perceived benefits from interventions and engagements with children and young people deemed to be possibly at risk.

Overall, these types of programme aim to encourage vital communities that should target a representative mix of age, gender and ethnicity. But some of these groups will be more at risk of criminal behaviour than others, and the following example considers the Youth Inclusion Programme (YIP) in being throughout England and Wales. This programme was previously run by the Youth Justice Board (YJB). The Youth Justice Board for England and Wales was an executive non-departmental public body which oversaw the youth justice system in England and Wales. Part of their work was to prevent offending and re-offending by children and young people under the age of 18, to ensure that custody for them is safe and secure and to try to address the causes of offending behaviour.

A range of early intervention and diversionary schemes that tackle the underlying problems, which exist in a young person's life and which may lead them to commit crime or anti-social behaviour, have been developed. The aim of the programme is to engage young people's interests from an early stage, increase their knowledge and consequently divert them from offending. It includes the YIP, which works with those young people who are most at risk of offending and runs positive activities that can open up new opportunities for them, as well as the Youth Inclusion and Support Panels, which help Young Offender Teams and other local and national agencies to identify the problems affecting each young person and tackle them in a targeted way.

Some schemes make use of restorative justice principles (discussed in more depth elsewhere in this book) in order to help young people understand the impact of offending and learn what behaviour is acceptable to their peers and the community. By influencing policy, identifying effective practice and commissioning research on risk factors and how to tackle them, the YJB supports the idea that the welfare needs of young people, be it education or accommodation, directly affect the likelihood that they will offend or commit anti-social behaviour.

Youth Inclusion Programme

YIPs, established in 2000, are tailor-made programmes for 8- to 17-year-olds who are identified as being at high risk of involvement in offending or anti-social behaviour. YIPs are also open to other young people in the local area. The programme operates throughout the most deprived/high-crime estates in England and Wales (for more information, visit www.yjb.gov.uk/en-gb/).

The aim of YIPs is to reduce youth crime and anti-social behaviour in neighbourhoods where they work. Young people on the YIP are identified through a number of different agencies including youth offending teams (YOTs), police, social services, local education authorities or schools and other local agencies. The programme gives young people somewhere safe to go where they can learn new skills, take part in activities with others and get help with their education and career guidance. Positive role models – the workers and volunteer mentors – help change young people's attitudes to education and crime.

Aims of each project are to:

- engage with a high proportion of the core group, especially those members deemed most at risk;

- address the risks identified by assessment;

- increase access to mainstream and specialist services, especially in relation to education, training and employment, for the young people involved;

- prevent young people in the programme from entering the criminal justice system, and to reduce offending of young people already in the system;

- intervene not just on an individual level but with communities and families (especially the parents of the core group).

An independent national evaluation of the first three years of YIPs found that:

- arrest rates for the 50 young people considered to be most at risk of crime in each YIP had been reduced by 65 per cent;

- of those who had offended before joining the programme, 73 per cent were arrested for fewer offences after engaging with a YIP;

- of those who had not offended previously but who were at risk, 74 per cent did not go on to be arrested after engaging with a YIP.

(Source: www.yjb.gov.uk/en-gb/)

Another approach to preventing young people from engaging in crime and disorder and providing an opportunity for direct engagement between police officers and young people is the Safer School Partnership (SSP).

Safer School Partnerships

SSP programme enables local agencies to address significant behavioural and crime-related issues in and around a school. A result of the YJB's proposal to develop a new policing model for schools, the SSP programme was launched as a pilot in September 2002 and brought into mainstream policy in March 2006. Initially, SSPs provided a focused approach to address the high level of crime and anti-social behaviour committed in and around schools in some areas – crime committed by and against children and young people. Broader benefits have since been recognised by everyone involved, including improved community cohesion, a stronger sense of citizenship among children and an increased quality of life and opportunities for young people, their families and the wider community around the school. All schools involved in the SSP initiative have a police officer based in their school.

The school-based officer works with school staff and other local agencies:

- to reduce victimisation, criminality and anti-social behaviour within the school and its community;

- on whole-school approaches to behaviour and discipline;

- to identify and work with children and young people at risk of becoming victims or offenders;

- to ensure the full-time education of young offenders (a proven preventative factor in keeping young people away from crime);

- to support vulnerable children and young people through periods of transition, such as the move from primary to secondary school;

- to create a safer environment for children to learn in.

(Source: www.yjb.gov.uk/en-gb/)

Close working between police and schools is crucial to keeping children in education, off the streets and away from a life of crime. There are now over 450 SSPs operating throughout England and Wales, with police officers and community support officers based in selected schools. A continued growth in the set-up of SSPs is being demonstrated nationally as schools, police forces, YOTs, health services and local authorities engage in this highly effective method of working.

CHAPTER SUMMARY

This chapter has attempted to make the reader consider police and youth engagement from a slightly different perspective. It places engagement activities such as pre-school interventions, youth initiatives, etc. within the wider context of the idea of social crime prevention and attempts to support crime-resistant communities through social activities. By understanding these wider processes, the fact that the police are involved in such activities should now be seen as important. Despite the fact that these measures are difficult to assess and are long term in nature, the savings and benefits for society in general are enormous.

At a more direct interactional level, the latter part of this chapter has attempted to explain in part the viewing young people as being problematic by the way in which we tend to see those who are different as 'others', not like 'us' and therefore ascribed negative identities. Consequently, how we react and deal with individuals in this group of 'others', by misuse of discretion perhaps in the case of the police, can be tainted by pre-conceived ideas. All social interactions and engagements are complex, none more so than between the police and young people, but it is vital that the police have a good relationship with young people if they are to maintain the support of communities in the years to come.

FURTHER READING

Allen, J, Edmonds, S, Patterson, A, and Smith, D (2006) *Policing and the Criminal Justice System: Public Confidence Perceptions: Findings from the 2004/05 British Crime Survey.* London: Home Office. Available at http://rds.homeoffice.gov.uk/rds/pdfs06/rdsolr0706.pdf

Brantingham, P J and Faust, F L (1976) A Conceptual Model of Crime Prevention. *Crime and Delinquency*, **22**: 284–96.

Bright, J (1997) *Turning the Tide, Crime Community and Prevention.* London: Demos.

Brown, S (1998) *Understanding Youth and Crime.* Buckingham: Open University Press.

Raban, J (1991) *Hunting Mister Heartbreak.* London: Pan.

Reiner, R (2000) *The Politics of the Police*, 3rd edition. London: Harvester Wheatsheaf.

Rogers, C (2006) *Crime Reduction Partnerships.* Oxford: Oxford University Press.

Rogers, C (2008) *Leadership Skills for Police.* Oxford: Oxford University Press.

Wedlock, E (2006) *Crime and Cohesive Communities.* London: Home Office. Available online at http://rds.homeoffice.gov.uk/rds/pdfs06/rdsolr1906.pdf

REFERENCES

Allen, J, Edmonds, S, Patterson, A and Smith, D (2006) *Policing and the Criminal Justice System: Public Confidence Perceptions: Findings from the 2004/05 British Crime Survey.* London: Home Office. Available online at http://rds.homeoffice.gov.uk/rds/pdfs06/rdsolr0706.pdf

Brantingham, P J and Faust, F L (1976) A Conceptual Model of Crime Prevention. *Crime and Delinquency*, **22**: 284–96.

Bright, J (1991) Crime Prevention: The British Experience in Stenson, K and Cowell, T (eds) *The Politics of Crime Control.* London: Sage.

Brown, S (1998) *Understanding Youth and Crime.* Buckingham: Open University Press.

Raban, J (1991) *Hunting Mister Heartbreak.* London: Pan.

Reiner, R (2000) *The Politics of the Police* (3rd Edition). London: Harvester Wheatsheaf.

Rogers, C (2006) *Crime Reduction Partnerships.* Oxford: Oxford University Press.

Rogers, C (2008) *Leadership Skills for Police.* Oxford, Oxford University Press.

Wedlock, E (2006) *Crime and Cohesive Communities.* London: Home Office. Available online at http://rds.homeoffice.gov.uk/rds/pdfs06/rdsolr1906.pdf

www.communities.gov.uk/publications/communities/whatworks (website with free download regarding community cohesion).

www.dse.vic.gov.au/DSE/nrenpa.nsf/LinkView/095F91662D4508DBCA2574A9001BAF26F 0DDF44B84631C6ECA2574DD0005E5D3 (The Good Neighbourhood Programme, Victoria, Australia).

www.ncjrs.gov/html/ojjdp/2000_10_1/contents.html (details regarding the Perry Pre-School Initiative).

www.yjb.gov.uk/en-gb/ (The Youth Justice Board).

7 Young people as suspects: the 'appropriate adult'

CHAPTER OBJECTIVES

By the end of this chapter you should be able to:

- summarise the conditions of juvenile detention at the police station;
- describe the responsibilities and rights of the appropriate adult;
- understand the difficulties in defining the role of the appropriate adult and identify some of the influences on our understanding of the role;
- identify some of the criticisms of the role and practices of appropriate adults.

LINKS TO STANDARDS

The material in this chapter links to the Skills for Justice, National Occupational Standards Policing and Law Enforcement.

CJ201	Interview suspects in relation to priority and volume investigations.
CJ202	Interview suspects in relation to serious and complex investigations.
POL 2H2	Interview suspects.

Introduction

In short, the purpose of the 'appropriate adult' is to provide 'advice and assistance' to juvenile and mentally vulnerable detainees at the police station (Home Office, 2008a, Code C, para 3.18b). However, beyond this, the role of the appropriate adults, in terms of the aims of the role, how they should act and who is the best person to perform this role, is somewhat unclear. This chapter provides you with an overview of the key issues surrounding the appropriate adult, provides you with a number of tasks to encourage reflection and debate and develops your research skills.

Overview of the conditions of juvenile detention at the police station

Before moving on to consider the appropriate adult further, it is useful to summarise how the conditions of police detention are expected to differ for adults and juveniles. Although the Police and Criminal Evidence Act 1984 (PACE) has been subject to a recent review, the results of which are still not known (see Pierpoint, submitted), at the time of writing, it is the most comprehensive and influential statute defining police powers and safeguards for suspects. It is accompanied by detailed procedures in the Codes of Practice including Code C which regulates detention and questioning of detainees, including some special provisions for juveniles. According to Code C, a juvenile is someone who appears to be under the age of 17 years. There are some requirements for the detention and questioning of detainees which are common to adults and juveniles (although research shows that sometimes there may be differences in their experiences – see for example, Phillips and Brown, 1998; Pierpoint, 2004) including the following.

- A custody record must be opened as soon as practicable for each arrestee.
- The custody officer must monitor the conditions of custody (e.g. bedding, sanitation, clothing, refreshment, exercise and medical treatment) and record all this in the custody record.
- Periodic reviews of detention must be carried out to consider whether detention is still justified.
- Interviews must usually be audio (or visually) recorded.
- Detainees have the rights to free legal advice, to consult the Codes of Practice and to have someone informed.

However, there are additional requirements when it comes to the detention and questioning of a juvenile.

- The person responsible for the juvenile's welfare must be informed that the juvenile has been arrested and of his/her whereabouts.
- A juvenile should not be placed in a police cell/cell with an adult.
- An appropriate adult should be present at the stages (discussed in the next section).

Responsibilities of the appropriate adult

The presence of an appropriate adult is required when the detainee is:

- informed of his or her rights above;
- cautioned;
- interviewed;

- subject to an identification procedure (e.g. fingerprinted);

- intimately or strip searched;

- given a reprimand or final warning or charged;

- made to give a urine or non-intimate sample.

The appropriate adult also has certain rights, such as to request legal advice on behalf of the juvenile and to consult the custody record.

During police interviews, appropriate adults *are not expected to act simply as an observer; and the purpose of their presence is to: advise the person being interviewed; observe whether the interview is being conducted properly and fairly; facilitate communication with the person being interviewed* (Home Office, 2008a, Code C, para 11.17). It has been argued that this definition is ambiguous and contradictory (Pierpoint, 2006a).

REFLECTIVE TASK

- *Skim read the documents below. What are the similarities and differences in the role of the appropriate adult as described in them?*

    - *PACE Code C 2008 para 11.17*

    - *Crime and Disorder Act 1998 s.38*

    - *Guidance for Appropriate Adults on the Home Office website*

    - *Appropriate Adult Checklist (Spencer, 2001, p 8)*

- *What does this tell you about the role of the appropriate adult?*

- *From these documents, what do you think the main aim of the appropriate adult is?*

PRACTICAL TASK

- *Search for legal cases which involve discussion of the appropriate adult?*

- *What do they tell you about the role of the appropriate adult?*

Brief history of the appropriate adult

Although it is possible to point to many influences in the development of the role of the appropriate adult (Pierpoint, 2006b), much of the roots of the role can be found in the Confait case 1975–76 (Blackie, 1996). In this case, three youths were wrongly convicted of the murder of Maxwell Confait in South East

London based on their false confessions made under oppressive interviewing. In the subsequent Fisher Inquiry, which investigated the police's handling of the Confait case, the first youth was assessed as being 'mentally subnormal', the second was 'highly suggestible' and the third was only 14 years old. The police had infringed the Judges' Rules, which attempted to regulate police interviewing at the time, on a number of counts, including the fact that neither the youths' parents/guardians nor other independent persons of the same sex had been present.

In response to the findings by the Fisher Inquiry and the widespread concerns about the 'consistent flouting' of the Judges' Rules by the police when investigating crime and interviewing suspects (Koffman, 1985, p 17), the Labour Government of the day established, in 1978, the Royal Commission on Criminal Procedure (RCCP). However, another stimulus for the establishment of the RCCP was the somewhat contradictory public concern that the police lacked the necessary powers to cull the rise in crime (Brown, 1997). The RCCP was tasked with providing a thorough review of criminal procedure with an eye to obtaining the correct 'balance' between crime control and due process (see Brown, 1997). Following hearing evidence from a range of bodies representing crime control and due process concerns and commissioning, a large number of research studies recommended that the Judges' Rules should be replaced with a statutory code of practice to achieve greater clarity. Most of the recommendations of the 1981 report were enacted in PACE and the accompanying Codes, including the requirement that an appropriate adult accompany the juvenile suspect during the key stages of police detention and questioning. Code of Practice C also recognised that: *Although juveniles or people who are mentally disordered or otherwise mentally vulnerable are often capable of providing reliable evidence, they may, without knowing or wishing to do so, be particularly prone in certain circumstances to provide information that may be unreliable, misleading or self-incriminating* (Home Office, 2008a, Code C, Note for guidance 11C).

Since the creation of the role of the appropriate adult in PACE, it has been subject to a number of revisions in some of the subsequent editions of the Codes and in the Crime and Disorder Act 1998. In the revised Codes, a number of categories of people have been excluded from acting as appropriate adults: solicitors and independent custody visitors, people who have received admissions, people who are suspected of involvement in or are victims or witnesses of the offence in question and estranged parents if the juvenile objects to their presence. The Crime and Disorder Act 1998 extended the appropriate adult's role to include being present at a reprimand or final warning. It also required local authorities to ensure the provision of appropriate adults for juveniles and provided that it was youth offending teams' (YOTs) duty to co-ordinate their provision.

Over the past 25 years, the role of the appropriate adult has been subject to a limited amount of academic research, discussed below, and two official reviews, including the Review of PACE completed in March 2010. As part of the review, the government published a series of proposals in August 2008 (Home Office, 2008b)

1. The role of the appropriate adult should be limited to those who have received adequate training.

2. Parents, guardians or other relatives or friends of the suspect should be asked to attend the police station but their attendance should not be critical to progressing the investigation.

3. Extend the role of appropriate adult to act as a facilitator between the police and the parent, guardian etc.

4. Strongly promote the continued use of the trained volunteer and encourage the benefits to be achieved from using professional appropriate adult agencies.

5. Give a statutory role to police authorities to ensure that an effective appropriate adults' scheme is operating in their police area in conjunction with maintaining the requirements under the Crime and Disorder Act 1998 which places a statutory duty on local authorities to provide youth justice services to such extent as is appropriate for their area.

6. Development of local protocols with voluntary schemes on attendance and response times, with social services' departments and service level agreements with commercial companies.

7. Extend access to appropriate adults for those in custody from under 17 to under 18.

8. Consider the potential for appropriate adult support through the CJS process.

9. Provide access to an appropriate adult during voluntary interviews.

10. Scope the potential for developing a national support structure for appropriate adults and custody visitors on recruitment and retention, communications, learning the lessons and monitoring and accountability.

Figure 7.1 Government's original proposals for appropriate adults

including ten proposals in relation to the appropriate adult as shown in Figure 7.1 above.

The summary of responses and a table of proposed legislative changes and other work were finally published in March 2010 (Home Office, 2010). The proposals made here in respect of the appropriate adult were significantly reduced in number – the only proposed legislative change was to change the age of juvenile from under 17 to under 18 years. However, in the wake of a new government, it is unclear which proposals will be taken forward if any.

REFLECTIVE TASK

• *Considering where the role of the appropriate adult came from, do you think the main aim of the appropriate adult is the same aim as you identified in the previous reflective task?*

Who can and who does act as an appropriate adult?

Under Code C, an appropriate adult for a juvenile can be:

- a parent or guardian;

- a social worker;

- another responsible adult aged 18 years or over who is not employed by the police.

For a mentally vulnerable detainee, an appropriate adult can be a relative, guardian or other person responsible for their care, someone experienced in dealing with mentally disordered or mentally vulnerable people but who is not employed by the police or another responsible adult aged 18 years.

Phillips and Brown's (1998) study, which comprised observation for five weeks at ten police stations, found that parents and social workers acted as appropriate adults in 63 per cent and 20 per cent of cases, respectively ($n = 599$). Volunteers (or, more precisely, members from local panels of appropriate adults) were used in two per cent of cases. However, it is likely that this percentage would now be substantially larger since, as discussed above, the Crime and Disorder Act 1998 required local authorities to ensure the provision of appropriate adults for juveniles, and Home Office guidance on the Act recommended that they use volunteers for their appropriate adult provision (Home Office, 1998). A postal survey of YOT managers in 2000 found that volunteers were used as appropriate adults in 50 per cent of their areas ($n = 120$, data missing in 30 cases) (Pierpoint, 2004). This move followed various calls for the use of volunteers as appropriate adults by, for example, the Audit Commission and Home Office Appropriate Adult Review Group (Audit Commission, 1996; Home Office, 1995). Arguments made in favour of using volunteers, some more convincingly than others, have related to the potentially increased availability of appropriate adults, cost and time saving accrued to YOTs, the notion of good citizenship and improved police-community relations (see Pierpoint, 2004).

It is also likely that since the Crime and Disorder Act 1998 provided that it was YOTs' duty to co-ordinate the provision of appropriate adults that YOT workers (whether they be social workers or not) have increasingly filled the role. A final category of appropriate adults is the paid appropriate adults employed by private companies and contracted by YOTs to provide appropriate adult service. Unfortunately, there is no research which establishes the extent to which people from these two categories are used, but numerous such private companies are listed online.

PRACTICAL TASK

- *Search the Internet to see if there are any private companies or voluntary agencies providing appropriate adult services in your area. Do they seem to be providing similar or different services?*

Research on the practices of appropriate adult

The section will identify what is known about what three kinds of appropriate adult – parents, social workers and volunteers – do in practice. Perhaps the most important stage in understanding what appropriate adults do in practice is the contribution that they make during the police interview, and this is what the section will focus on.

Parents

Evans (1993, p 39) found that in 75 per cent (*n* = 98) of interviews, *parents and other appropriate adults who attended interviews* made no contribution whatsoever. Evans (1993) found that, when parents did contribute, they were unsupportive in 50 per cent of cases (*n* = 66). He found that parents, when unsupportive, generally put pressure on their children to confess, or told the police that they washed their hands of their children or that their children should have known better. For example, Evans (1993, p 40) cited a father commenting: *It's against the law, it's as simple as that. As a 16 year old he or she should have more sense.*

Other parents perceive their role as one of 'assisting' the police in extracting a confession, even to the extent of chastising their children. According to Gudjonsson (1993), it is not unusual for parents to resort to intimidatory tactics. Dixon et al. (1990, p 119) referred to an incident that they observed in one of the three subdivisions (covering the contrasting geographical areas of city centre, outer estate and rural/seaside/market town mix) in a medium-sized force in the north of England, in which a mother promised to 'get my fist round his lug'. Irving and McKenzie (1989) cited a similar case of a young suspect's uncle who saw his role as expediting a confession.

Bean (1997) suggested that there are two types of parent appropriate adult: the aforementioned 'wait till I get you home and I'll wallop you' type and the 'don't tell them anything' type. Indeed, Brown et al. (1992, p 73) observed that some parents *vehemently took sides against the police*. Bucke and Brown (1997, p 11) characterised the disposition of 5 per cent of family members as 'hostile/unsupportive' towards the police.

In contrast to Evans' (1993) findings, Bucke and Brown (1997, p 11), from their observations in 25 police stations in ten police forces, characterised the demeanour of only 8 per cent of family members as 'hostile/unsupportive' towards the suspect (*n* = 415). They found that most frequently family members were 'neutral' (30 per cent), followed by 'cooperative/supportive' (26 per cent) towards the suspect (*n* = 415). Nevertheless, most of the evidence available suggests that parents' contributions are infrequent and unsupportive.

Social workers

Social workers have also been found to make little contribution to the police interview. Evans (1993, p 40) found that, in 18 of the 29 cases (63 per cent) in which social workers attended, the police used persuasive techniques and obtained a confession, without any interjection from the social workers. Evans and Rawstorne (1994) also found that according to the interviewing officers who they interviewed, social workers took no or little active part in interviews.

When social workers do take an active role in the police interview, they may execute the appropriate adult role in accordance with either control or welfare ideologies. Dixon (1990) suggested that there is a tension between control and welfare ideologies in social work. If social workers operate according to the control ideology, they may attempt to inculcate moral responsibility in the suspect for what he or she is alleged to have done. For example, a social worker may be inclined to 'encourage' the suspect to confess, whereas it may be in the suspect's welfare or legal interests to advise him or her to exercise their right to silence (albeit curtailed) (Kay and Quao, 1987). Besides, juveniles are likely to consider social workers to be instruments of control (Brown, 1997). As Dixon (1990, p 123) pointed out, the social worker *may well be perceived by that juvenile as part of the system which is detaining and will probably punish him/her*.

In contrast, Bucke and Brown (1997) found that social workers tended to provide a more calm and dispassionate approach than family members. They found that the majority of social workers (45 per cent, $n = 211$) were 'cooperative/supportive' towards the suspect. The majority of social workers (60 per cent, $n = 211$) were also 'cooperative/supportive' towards the police. These points are underlined by the examples cited by Bucke and Brown (1997). For instance, one observer reported of a social worker: *Very quiet but cooperative with officers. Offered to bring the boy back to answer his bail. Not angry or reproachful towards the boy – very at ease* (as cited by Bucke and Brown, 1997, p 15).

Volunteers

Pierpoint (2006a) conducted a survey of volunteer appropriate adult call outs to the police station. She asked volunteers to complete a questionnaire after each time they had been called out. According to the questionnaire data, in 35 per cent of interviews, volunteers contributed ($n = 125$, data missing for two cases). However, in the remaining 65 per cent of interviews, the volunteer appropriate adults reported not to have said anything ($n = 125$, data missing for two cases). It is possible that contribution was not necessary and that the interviews were properly conducted and communication flowed well without the volunteers' assistance. It is also possible that the volunteers failed to report their contribution or advised the young person outside the interview. On the other hand, it is possible that the interview was not conducted fairly or properly and the volunteers failed to contribute.

As shown in Table 7.1 overleaf, where volunteers contributed in interviews, key contributions were, despite the frequent presence of a legal adviser, dealing with unfair questioning, checking comprehension of questions and processes, such as the caution, and comforting the suspect. For volunteers, unfair questioning seemed

Table 7.1 Nature of volunteers' contributions (multiple response)

Nature of contribution	No. of responses	Per cent of interviews
Pointed out police questioning unfair	8	19
Checked young person understood question(s)	7	16
Stopped interview	6	14
Checked young person understood caution	5	12
Comforted young person	5	12
Asked police for clarification of special warning	4	9
Advised young person to take legal advice	3	7
Asked for question(s) to be clarified	3	7
Reminded young person that they had elected 'no comment' interview	3	7
Other	14	32

Note: $N = 43$ (only cases in which volunteers contributed)

to be threatening or confusing, which sometimes resulted in volunteers stopping interviews. For example, one volunteer appropriate adult reported:

> *Interviewing officer read out a final set of questions that seemed quite threatening. Following a special warning – that is not legally binding young person looked confused. I asked for the questions to be interpreted into plain English and followed up by asking the young person if they understood. They did not and asked for further legal advice. The interview was stopped and we all discussed what the questions' context is in an interview.*

In sum, volunteers, who participated in Pierpoint's (2006a) survey, reported a higher level of contribution than was observed by Evans (1993) for 'parents and other appropriate adults' but not social workers alone. When the three groups did contribute, their contributions were often very different, and this is one of the key criticisms of the appropriate adult.

REFLECTIVE TASK

- *How much confidence can we have in the research findings above? What are the limitations of the research studies discussed above? Why do you think some of the research findings are inconsistent?*

- *Why do you think that so many appropriate adults did not say anything in the police interviews?*

- *Why do you think some appropriate adults act differently from others?*

- *Who do you think makes the best appropriate adult and why?*

Criticisms of the appropriate adult

As discussed above, over the years, the appropriate adult has been the subject of a number of official reviews and research studies. The main criticisms made by the various reviews and by academics have been the:

- lack of contribution in police interviews by some appropriate adults and the different practices of parents, social workers and volunteers in the role;

- treatment of 17-year-olds as adults and the fact that they are not required to be accompanied by an appropriate adult;

- difficulties and delays in obtaining appropriate adults;

- ambiguity and contradictory nature of the definition of the appropriate adult in the PACE Codes;

- lack of a national policy and guidance for appropriate adult services.

Some of these criticisms have been discussed above. The PACE Review, also discussed above, did refer to increasing the age of a juvenile to under 18 years and developing a national approach for appropriate adult and sought suggestions on how to raise their input and improve the quality of contact with suspects, but how the new government is going to take this forward is yet to be seen.

> REFLECTIVE TASK
>
> - *From what you have read, do you think that these criticisms are fair?*
>
> - *If so, what should be done to respond to them?*

C H A P T E R   S U M M A R Y

This chapter started by arguing that the role of the appropriate adult is somewhat unclear and ambiguous. The discussion above, together with the further sources that you will have collected if you have undertaken the reflective and practical tasks diligently, will have highlighted that our understanding of the role is shaped by its history, various official definitions, case law and interpretations of the different appropriate adults themselves. The practices of three categories of appropriate adult have been discussed and the key criticisms of the role highlighted. We await what will happen under the new government with anticipation.

FURTHER READING

Home Office (2010) *PACE Review: Summary of Responses to the Public Consultation on the Review of the Police and Criminal Evidence Act 1984*, March 2010. Available online at http://webarchive.nationalarchives.gov.uk/20100418065544/http://www.homeoffice.gov.uk/documents/cons-2008-pace-review/PACE-review-20102835.pdf?view=Binary

Pierpoint, H (2004) A Survey on Volunteer Appropriate Adult Services. *Youth Justice*, **4**(1): 32–45.

Pierpoint, H (2006a) Reconstructing the Role of the Appropriate Adult in England and Wales. *Criminology and Criminal Justice: The International Journal*, **6**(2): 219–38.

REFERENCES

Audit Commission (1996) *Misspent Youth*. London: Audit Commission.

Bean, P (1997) Awareness of the Appropriate Adult. *Justice of the Peace and Local Government*, **161**(15), 355–56.

Blackie, I (1996) Appropriate Adults. *National Association for the Protection from Sexual Abuse of Adults and Children with Learning Difficulties Bulletin*, June, 3–7.

Brown, D (1997) *PACE Ten Years On: A Review of the Research. Home Office Research Study; 155*. London: Home Office.

Brown, D, Ellis, T and Larcombe, K (1992) *Changing the Code: Police Detention under the Revised PACE Codes of Practice (HORS 129)*. London: HMSO.

Bucke, T and Brown, D (1997) *In Police Custody: Police Powers and Suspects' Rights under the Revised PACE Codes of Practice (HORS 174)*. London: HMSO.

Dixon, D (1990) Young Person Suspects and the Police and Criminal Evidence Act, in Freestone, D (ed) *Children and the Law: Essays in Honour of Professor H. K. Bevan*. Hull: Hull University Press.

Dixon, D, Bottomley, K, Coleman, C, Gill, M and Wall, D (1990) Safeguarding the Rights of Suspects in Police Custody. *Policing and Society*, **1**, 115–40.

Evans, R (1993) *The Conduct of Police Interviews with Young People* (Royal Commission on Criminal Justice Research Study No. 8). London: HMSO.

Evans, R and Rawstorne, S (1994) The Protection of Vulnerable Suspects (A Report to the Home Office Research and Planning Unit). Unpublished.

Gudjonsson, G. (1993) Confession Evidence, Psychological Vulnerability and Expert Testimony. *Journal of Community and Applied Social Psychology*, **3**, 117–29.

Home Office (1995) *Appropriate Adults: Report of Review Group*. London: HMSO.

Home Office (1998) *Inter-departmental Circular on Establishing Youth Offending Teams* (22 December 1998). Available online at http://www.homeoffice.gov.uk/docs/yotcirc2.html/ (accessed 24 June 2003).

Home Office (2008a) *Police and Criminal Evidence Act 1984 – PACE Codes*. Available online at http://webarchive.nationalarchives.gov.uk/20100418065544/http://police.homeoffice.gov.uk/operational-policing/powers-pace-codes/pace-code-intro/ (accessed 13 May 2010).

Home Office (2008b) *PACE Review: Government Proposals in Response to the Review of the Police and Criminal Evidence Act 1984*, August 2008. Available online at http://webarchive.nationalar-chives.gov.uk/20100418065544/http://homeoffice.gov.uk/documents/cons-2008-pace-review/cons-2008-pace-review-pdf2835.pdf?view=Binary (accessed 13 May 2010)

Home Office (2010) *PACE Review: Summary of Responses to the Public Consultation on the Review of the Police and Criminal Evidence Act 1984 March 2010*. Available online at http://webarchive.nationalarchives.gov.uk/20100418065544/http://www.homeoffice.gov.uk/docu-ments/cons-2008-pace-review/PACE-review-20102835.pdf?view=Binary (accessed 13 May 2010)

Irving, B and MacKenzie, I K (1989) *Police Interrogation: The Effects of the Police and Criminal Evidence Act 1984*. London: Police Foundation.

Kay, N and Quao, S (1987) To Be or Not To Be an 'Appropriate Adult'. *Community Care*, **9** July, 20–2.

Koffman, L (1985) Safeguarding the Rights of Citizens, in Baxter, J and Koffman, L (eds) *Police: The Constitution and the Community*. Oxon: Professional Books Limited.

Phillips, C and Brown, D, with the assistance of James, Z and Goodrich, P (1998) *Entry into the Criminal Justice System: A Survey of Police Arrests and Their Outcomes (HORS 185)*. London: Home Office.

Pierpoint, H (2004) A Survey on Volunteer Appropriate Adult Services. *Youth Justice*, **4**(1), 32–45.

Pierpoint, H (2006a) Reconstructing the Role of the Appropriate Adult in England and Wales. *Criminology and Criminal Justice: The International Journal*, **6**(2), 219–38.

Pierpoint, H (2006b) Appropriate Practice? A Study of the Role and Co-ordination of Volunteer Appropriate Adults for Young Suspects. Unpublished thesis (PhD), Faculty of Social Science and Business, University of Plymouth.

Pierpoint, H (submitted) Extending and Professionalising the Role of the Appropriate Adult. Submitted to Criminology and Criminal Justice: *The International Journal* (14/05/10).

Spencer, Y (2001) At the Police Station: The Role of the Appropriate Adult. *Childright*, **177**, supp 1–8.

www.appropriateadult.org.uk/ (National Appropriate Adult Network).

www.homeoffice.gov.uk/ (Home Office).

www.yjb.gov.uk/ (Youth Justice Board).

8 Young people as witnesses

CHAPTER OBJECTIVES

By the end of this chapter you should have:

- gained an understanding of how important landmark cases and reviews have influenced the development of law and practice relating to young people as witnesses;
- gained an understanding of the underpinning legal concepts of reliability, credibility and compellability;
- gained an appreciation of the major areas of continuing research that influence legislation and policy dealing with young people as witnesses;
- understood the type of information that will be needed if the special measures available to young people as witnesses in the criminal courts are to be successfully applied for;
- understood how the special measures might be used to mitigate the effects of the judicial process on the young vulnerable witness and enhance their evidence;
- a clear view of how the guidance associated with the interviewing of young people as witnesses links directly to the basic legal concepts, and to the special measures available for young people as witnesses;
- understood the importance of considering the links between the law, guidance and practice at all times, when dealing with young witnesses, if you are to obtain the best evidence.

LINKS TO STANDARDS

This chapter is linked to Skills for Justice, National Occupational Standards Policing and Law Enforcement (2010).

BE2 (CJC 102)	Provide initial support to victims, survivors and witnesses and assess their need for further support.
CJ101	Interview victims and witnesses in relation to priority and volume investigations.
CJ102	Interview victims and witnesses in relation to serious and complex investigations.
POL 2H1	Interview victims and witnesses.

Introduction

This chapter considers the legal and developmental concepts and issues that affect children as witnesses. These issues affect how young people's evidence is obtained and received within the criminal justice system and within the child safeguarding arena and its associated procedures. The chapter provides an overview of the basic issues of reliability, credibility and compellability and links those issues to legislation and investigative guidance that is utilised by professional practitioners who deal with young people as witnesses.

Witnesses to, and victims of, all types of crime come from all age groups, including young people, even the youngest of infants are victims of crimes. There are many highly emotive landmark cases involving children as victims of crime, and there have also been a large number of inquiries into the circumstances of many of those cases. Those inquiries have had a direct influence on the way that such cases are now investigated and the way that courts deal with the evidence produced during such investigations. This is a complex area, and the development of procedures and guidance regarding children within the 'safeguarding' arena is linked with the developments in how young witnesses are dealt with in the criminal justice system.

This chapter refers to enquiries into landmark and often tragic cases involving children as victims but will focus on the concept of young people as witnesses. In order to understand the present position regarding young witnesses, a basic appreciation of some legal concepts regarding witnesses, and of the research that informs our understanding of child memory and recall, is needed. Some appreciation of the historical context is also helpful as it allows a deeper understanding of how and why the present law and guidance has been constructed. The historical context is complex in itself because landmark cases and inquiries have influenced not only the law but the procedures and guidance that agencies, including the police, adhere to. The law and the guidance to investigators provide a framework for investigators to work within when they are dealing with young witnesses; this chapter will outline how the law and guidance work in practice. Each case will include many different variables: the nature of the case, the nature of the witness and the nature of the accused; because of these variables, the application of the law and the associated guidance has to be implemented with a close understanding of what both are trying to achieve. Associated with many investigations involving children are the 'safeguarding procedures' addressed elsewhere in this book; both chapters together will provide a clear understanding of this complex area of police work.

The crimes that have driven the development of the law and associated investigative procedures and guidance regarding vulnerable victims and children in particular have distinct characteristics. These crimes have been grave and highlight the vulnerability and isolation of children if they are betrayed by those upon whom they depend. The crimes are usually 'private' in nature, with only the offender(s) and the young person being present. This characteristic focuses attention on the victim as a witness. In some cases, involving infants, the child becomes the evidence. Rather than what the child may have experienced, being the evidence presented to the court the child becomes a body that can produce substantive scientific evidence, for example, the products of the medical examination and photographs. The child can almost become an exhibit in the court process. This is inevitable as infants have very limited communication abilities. As children grow and develop, the ability to communicate and understand develops too. Although these developments may be measured, they do not occur at the same rate in all children. An understanding of that development is important if investigations involving children and young people are to be effective in terms of producing usable evidence, and if the investigators are to be able to make judgements about the best way to protect the child from being damaged by the investigative and judicial processes, while at the same time ensure the rights of the accused are also protected.

Witness credibility, reliability and compellability

'Credibility' and 'reliability' are important legal concepts, and they are particularly important when dealing with young witnesses.

The concept of 'credibility' is concerned with how believable a witness is. In any criminal court, there are people who carry out the role of judging fact. In the magistrate's court, the role is fulfilled by the magistrate or district judge, and in the crown courts, the fact finders are the members of the jury. Credibility is judged by the fact finders. How they perceive the witness and the credibility of the witness will be influenced by how the witness acts and by what the witness says. Individual fact finders may have different views of what makes a witness credible. The ability to describe a crime clearly and dispassionately can be seen by some to provide evidence of credibility, while for others such ability might demonstrate that the witness could not have been a victim, as they show no emotional involvement.

REFLECTIVE TASK

Consider your own experiences of how different people act in similar circumstances. What other information and knowledge is needed for you to accurately judge a person's credibility? Think about what this might mean in assessing the credibility of any witness.

The concept of reliability is concerned with the accuracy of the witness, and this is a well-researched area. Ray Bull's Children and the Law 2001 provides you with a snapshot of some of the research and some of the areas where research has taken place. Reliability has always been an issue for the judicial process, an issue that has had an impact on both adult and young witnesses. Reliability is the ability to remember and to recall memories. It is an area that continues to be researched in both adults and the young. The reliability of young witnesses is complicated by the natural development and growth of the child concerned because growth, age and development change the abilities of the witness. As well as the issues of memory and recall, children are different from adults because of the relationship they have with adults. Children in general will regard adults differently from their peers; they will have relied upon adults for protection and nurturing and that reliance influences what witnesses may say in response to questioning. The methods and techniques used to interview young witnesses, and other vulnerable witnesses, who may be open to suggestion, have been developed to try to improve the reliability of the evidence they provide. 'Achieving Best Evidence in Criminal Proceeding' (Home Office, 2007) contains guidance for interviewers that helps to minimise the risks of suggestion influencing the testimony of young witnesses. Direct suggestion, such as the use of leading questions, as a technique in interview is easy to understand, but due to the relationship that children have with adults, there are other more subtle forms of suggestion that have been identified. Children usually try to please adults and will consider the reactions of the interviewer; there is, therefore, a danger that positive or encouraging reactions can be interpreted by the young witness as a reward for a 'correct' answer (Bruck et al., 2001).

Reliability of witnesses has always been an issue for the courts, and for certain criminal trials, the judicial system has put in place rules to try to improve reliability, and so protect the accused from unreliable or malicious testimony. Prior to 1991, the common law required that judges sitting in all sexual offence cases warn juries, regardless of the age of the victim, of the absence of corroboration and the dangers of convicting on such uncorroborated evidence. This blanket warning was particularly pertinent in child sexual abuse cases, where corroboration is difficult to come by. The warning coupled with the fact that research into the issues influencing young witness reliability was not as advanced as it now is led to a situation where it was particularly difficult to utilise the oral evidence of young people who had been the victims of very serious crimes. Research such as that referred to above has allowed a much better understanding of the reliability of young witnesses and the issues that influence reliability.

Both the concepts of reliability and credibility are linked to the legal issues of competence and compellability that impact on all victims and witnesses, but they impact on young witnesses in particular ways. The general rule is that 'all people are competent and all competent witnesses are compellable' as s53 of the Youth Justice and Criminal Evidence Act 1999 states:

> *At every stage in criminal proceedings all persons are (whatever their age) competent to give evidence.*

There are exceptions and conditions that apply to some people, including young people. The particular exceptions and conditions that apply to young people are important to understand as they provide a basis and context that helps in the understanding of the Home Office guidance to interviewers and investigators contained in 'Achieving Best Evidence in Criminal Proceedings' (Home Office, 2007). The Youth Justice and Criminal Evidence Act 1999, section 55, addresses the issue of 'sworn evidence', that is, evidence that is given under oath. To give evidence under oath, a witness must understand the gravity of the oath and the responsibility to tell the truth, and the act determines that a child who has not attained the age of 14 years cannot give 'sworn evidence', and if aged between 14 and 17 years, then the child must have

> *Sufficient appreciation of the solemnity of the occasion and of the particular responsibility to tell the truth which is involved in taking the oath.*

However, s55 goes on to say:

> *If he is able to give intelligible testimony, (he) will be presumed to have sufficient appreciation of those matters if no evidence to the contrary is adduced (by any party).*

Children under the age of 14 can provide 'unsworn evidence' on condition that they can provide 'intelligible testimony', and this ability is determined by the judge (G v DPP 2 All ER 755). Although there is no set lower age limit, in practice, the younger a witness is, the harder it is likely to be for them to pass the 'intelligible testimony' test.

It is true that in general terms a child's competence to give evidence generally increases as they age; however, as all children develop at different rates, there can be no hard and fast rules that can be applied across the board. In practice, although young witnesses may be competent, it is important that initial investigators understand the practical implications of a young witness getting their testimony accepted as evidence. It is important for the interviewer of a child to understand the concepts of reliability, credibility and competence, and to understand how those concepts are likely to be tested in court. Within an investigative interview of a young witness, trained interviewers might test understanding of truth and wrongdoing and will also be in a position to make judgments regarding the 'intelligible testimony' test. It is also easier to understand how the judicial system and investigative agencies have adapted their practice and environments to the benefit of young witnesses if these basic concepts are understood.

R E F L E C T I V E   T A S K

Formulate a number of questions that would demonstrate young witnesses' understanding of truth, lies, right and wrong. Include in those questions one that would indicate the child's understanding of a serious wrong and a less serious wrong. In formulating the question, you will need to relate it to something the child witness is likely to understand or have experienced. For example, 'Tell me what would be a naughty thing to do'. Or 'if you have failed to do your homework because you were out with your friends, but you tell your teacher it was because you were ill, what does that say about your honesty?' In testing appreciation of seriousness of wrong, you could ask 'Some people sometimes tell 'fibs.' What is the difference between a 'fib' and a 'lie'.

Special measures and investigative practice

The special measures available to vulnerable witnesses under the Youth Justice and Criminal Evidence Act 1999 are described and examined in more detail later in this chapter, but they can be seen as part of legislative development that was initiated following the Investigation into the Cleveland Sexual Abuse Cases in 1987 (Butler-Sloss, 1988). This landmark case highlighted many shortcomings in how such cases were dealt with at the time, including the manner in which young witnesses and victims were interviewed and the knowledge of the interviewers about children and their development. The recommendations made included improving the training of interviewing techniques and working in a multi-agency environment.

Developments following the Butler-Sloss inquiry report included the 'Report of the Advisory Group on Video Evidence' (Pigot, 1989) which looked in detail at the evidence of young witnesses and how that evidence was gathered, presented and examined at court. In particular, it examined the concept of using video-recorded evidence and closed circuit television, both in the initial investigative process and then later in the presentation of the case to the courts. This report led to the Criminal Justice Act 1991 that allowed young witnesses, in carefully defined circumstances, to make use of the, then new, technology of video recording in the presentation of their evidence.

This was a significant first step towards the special measures that are now in place. The measures that have continued to develop have focused on providing an environment that is less intimidating to the vulnerable witness and enabling them to provide oral evidence. For the young witness, this has helped to change the view that young witnesses are a source of evidence as an object subject of forensic medical examination to one where they might provide acceptable oral testimony. The measures enable the court, in the correct legal circumstances, to avail themselves of the eyewitness testimony of witnesses, while mitigating the effect of that process upon the vulnerable.

It is important to understand that the court process is at the end of what can be a long and complicated investigative process, and the special measures available must not be considered in isolation, or as a stand-alone facility. In order for the special measures to be implemented, it is important that the initial investigative process is run with the special measures that are defined in the Youth Justice and Criminal Evidence Act 1999 in mind. Decisions about the vulnerability of the witness and the measures that may be needed to support the young witness need to be appreciated, if not made, at the initial stages of the investigation. Some of those decisions will be taken in the light of judgements made about competence, reliability and credibility as discussed previously, while others are informed by the Youth Justice and Criminal Evidence Act 1999 which defines 'vulnerability' and the rules governing eligibility for 'special measures'.

The Youth Justice and Criminal Evidence Act 1999 describes different categories of witnesses who are eligible for special measures. Section 16 deals specifically with witnesses who are eligible on the grounds of age in particular, and it states that:

1) *For the purposes of this Chapter a witness in criminal proceedings (other than the accused) is eligible for assistance by virtue of this section—*

    (a) *if under the age of 17 at the time of the hearing.*

While the act is clear about the age at which a young witness may be 'eligible' for assistance (special measures) and outlines 'eligibility', it does not give young people under the age of 17 either a 'right', or the courts an 'obligation' that is mandatory. Section 17 of the act outlines how witnesses may be eligible for assistance on grounds of fear or distress about testifying. Section 17(2) (3) and (4) of the Youth Justice and Criminal Evidence Act 1999 identifies the following factors that should be taken into account by the court when determining vulnerability:

   (a) *the nature and alleged circumstances of the offence to which the proceedings relate;*

   (b) *the age of the witness;*

   (c) *such of the following matters as appear to the court to be relevant, namely—*

       (i) *the social and cultural background and ethnic origins of the witness,*

       (ii) *the domestic and employment circumstances of the witness, and*

       (iii) *any religious beliefs or political opinions of the witness;*

   (d) *any behaviour towards the witness on the part of—*

       (i) *the accused,*

       (ii) *members of the family or associates of the accused, or*

       (iii) *any other person who is likely to be an accused or a witness in the proceedings.*

(3) *In determining that question the court must in addition consider any views expressed by the witness.*

(4) *Where the complainant in respect of a sexual offence is a witness in proceedings relating to that offence (or to that offence and any other offences), the witness is eligible for assistance in relation to those proceedings by virtue of this subsection unless the witness has informed the court of the witness' wish not to be so eligible by virtue of this subsection.*

Section 4 above allows a witness or victim make their own decision about whether they require to be considered for special measures.

In summary, at this stage of the process, where a young witness aged under 17 years is involved, then the court first determines vulnerability using the criteria outlined above within section 17(2) of the Criminal and Youth Justice Act 1991. If the court determines that the witness is indeed vulnerable, it must then consider the next step as outlined in Section 19 of the same act.

Under Section 19(2) of the legislation if the court *determines that the witness is eligible for assistance by virtue of section 16*, the court must then

(a) *determine whether any of the special measures available in relation to the witness (or any combination of them) would, in its opinion, be likely to improve the quality of evidence given by the witness; and*

(b) *if so—*

(i) *determine which of those measures (or combination of them) would, in its opinion, be likely to maximise so far as practicable the quality of such evidence.*

Although eligible by the age criteria laid out within the act (s16), a young person's entitlement to special measures is governed by how those special measures might improve the quality of the evidence. The act then requires that the court considers the specific measures available and which of those measures would achieve that improvement in quality. Although the special measures may mitigate the effect of the court process upon the young witness, they are primarily concerned with improving the quality of the evidence provided by the vulnerable witness. The process outlined within Sections 16, 17 and 19 of the act is applicable to vulnerable witnesses in general, as well as to those who qualify by age (under 17 years). It is important to understand that under these sections of the act, the access to special measures is described as 'eligibility', it is not an 'entitlement'. If an application is to be made to the court under these sections, the applying party will need to produce information that allows the court to determine which special measures might improve the quality of the evidence and how they might achieve that improvement.

REFLECTIVE TASK

Using the criteria outlined in Section 17(2) of the Youth Justice and Criminal Evidence Act 1999, consider what information and evidence could be produced to a court to allow a determination of 'vulnerability'.

The application of, and entitlement to, special measures is further developed in Section 21 of the same act which defines other circumstances under which special measures are an 'entitlement' for young witnesses. This section deals with child witnesses (as defined by Section 16(1)(a)) who are in need of 'special protection'. The eligibility for these 'special protective measures' is dependent on the nature of the offence which the child has witnessed or been a victim. The specific crimes are described within Sections 35 (3)(a)(b)(c) and (d). These crimes can be broadly classified as sexual offences, child protection offences and child abduction offences, and include in Section 35(d) offences that involve 'an assault on, or injury or a threat of injury to, any person.' The offences are serious and are very likely to include circumstances that will impact on the vulnerability of the child witness.

REFLECTIVE TASK

Consider the words 'special protective measures'. What does this description imply, and why might they be particularly relevant to the types of offences broadly out-lined above?

These special protective measures include video-recorded evidence in chief and cross-examination. Where a child is involved in one of the serious cases outlined in Section 35, the act directs that the court has an obligation to admit any recording made as evidence in chief (Section 27 refers) and that any evidence not given by means of video recording must be given by means of a live video link.

Section 27 of the act refers to the admission of a video recording of a child wit-ness as evidence in chief. The video-recorded interview is not taken 'under oath' but is accorded the same evidential weight as evidence taken 'under oath' directly in the court. Linked to this is Section 28 which allows for the cross-examination of a child witness to be similarly recorded and admitted in evidence. The special measures outlined in Sections 27 and 28 provide for the witness to be remote from the court room and remote from the accused. However, the act provides certain safeguards for the accused to protect their rights. The act states that the accused must be able to communicate with their legal representative and be able to see and hear the witness during the cross-examination. In addition, Section 28(2)a states *the judge or justices are able to see and hear the examination of the witness and to communicate with the persons in whose presence the recording is being made*.

While the use of CCTV during the court hearing in particular raises issues for the rights of the witness and the suspect in the case, it also brings into focus the tactics of presenting evidence and winning cases in an adversarial system. It is important to remember that the adversarial system of justice has been developed to test evidence; how that testing of evidence is carried out within the system includes the consideration of the best tactics and methods of presenting the evidence in order to gain the most beneficial effect of that evidence. This applies to both the prosecution and the defence cases, and each side will consider how it can 'win' the case.

In all cases, advocates and investigators need to consider the best way to present the evidence, but also the wider effects that the experience of testifying might have on the witness. Part of this consideration is how the experience will affect the delivery of the evidence, but there also needs to be consideration of the welfare of the witness. In cases where vulnerable witnesses, including the young, are involved, these considerations are more acute. Advocates and investigators need to consider what will achieve the best case result and what will the collateral implications be for the 'vulnerable witness'. To be able to judge those wider implications, information about the witness' abilities and particular vulnerabilities needs to be carefully assessed; it may be that the interviewer is in the best position to inform those assessments. Arguments are made that the impact of a witness live in court, delivering evidence face to face, is more powerful than the evidence delivered through the sanitising and distancing medium of CCTV. Part of that impact may well be the obvious emotional turmoil of the witness that is transmitted directly to the jury. (Goodman et al., 2001). The fact that the witness is in 'obvious emotional turmoil' can have a powerful effect on a court, but that 'turmoil' is unlikely to have a beneficial effect on the witness; the actual process of delivering live testimony to a court may increase those feelings and emotions and 'turmoil'.

There are also arguments about the delivery of witness testimony via CCTV impinging upon the rights of the accused to a fair trial under Article 6 of Human Rights Act 1998. This needs to be balanced against the rights of the victim to a fair trial under the same legislation. As well as the issues about rights of both victim and accused are the issues that arise about the court's function and the role that fact finders play in that system, be they professional judiciary or lay jurors. These issues revolve around the ability of those fact finders to reach the truth of the case. In these issues, the questions that need to be answered are: Does the use of CCTV interfere with the ability of the fact finder to judge the credibility of the witness? Does face-to-face evidence delivery enhance the ability of fact finders to judge the credibility of the witness? Linked to this the investigator needs to know what do fact finders use to judge the credibility of witnesses and are they reliable and accurate indicators of credibility? Do all fact finders draw the same conclusions from the same indicators? Goodman et al. (2001) present research and discuss the issues above in more depth.

REFLECTIVE TASK

Consider how the rights of the accused could be said to be infringed by using CCTV as a special measure to enhance witness testimony.

Consider how the rights of the victim are enhanced by using CCTV as a special measure to enhance witness testimony.

The protection of witnesses, including children, is extended further by Section 34 of the Youth Justice and Criminal Evidence Act 1999, which precludes the cross-examination of victims of sexual offences by their alleged assailant. The law requires the defendant in such cases to appoint a legal representative, and if they refuse, the court will consider appointing a representative for them.

All the measures distancing the vulnerable young witness from the accused need to be carefully considered in their application. The framing of the legislation provides checks and balances that address the rights of both the accused and the victim. It is important that students understand both sides of this argument. Comprehension of the arguments allows the student to attain a deeper understanding of the guidance that is contained in 'Achieving Best Evidence in Criminal Proceeding (Home Office, 2007), that is discussed later.

The specific measures outlined in Sections 27, 28 and 34 of the Youth Justice and Criminal Evidence Act 1999 are three of a number of special measures that are available to the court, other measures include the following.

Section 23 provides for screening of the witness from the view of the accused. The screening must allow the witness to be seen by judge, justices or jury and the legal representative of the accused.

Section 24 allows for evidence to be given by live television link, and again the provision that the televised witness must be viewable by judge, justices or jury and the legal representative of the accused.

Section 25 provides for evidence given in private in sexual offence proceedings and where the court has reasonable grounds for that any person other than the accused has sought, or will seek, to intimidate the witness in connection with testifying in the proceedings. This allows for the exclusion from court of everyone except the accused, legal representatives acting in the case, interpreter or other person appointed to assist the witness.

These measures under ss 23, 24, and 25 are aimed at mitigating the effect of direct contact between the witness and the accused. Where the allegation involves crimes that have 'intimidation' as a factor within them, these measures are useful to protect the witness from further intimidation that can be transmitted by presence and proximity.

Section 26 provides for the removal of wigs and gowns by judiciary and advocates during the witnesses testimony. This measure is aimed at reducing the formality and 'grandeur' of the court environment.

Section 29 deals with the examination of witnesses through an intermediary. The intermediary's function is to help in communication between the witness and the court including prosecution and defence; this might include helping the witness to understand questions and in conveying answers to questions to the court.

Section 30 allows aids to communication to be provided with such device as the court considers appropriate to aid communication with who witness may suffer from a disability or impairment.

REFLECTIVE TASK

Compare the measures available under Sections 23, 24, 25, 26, 29 and 30 with those available under Sections 27, 28 and 34. Which do you consider to be most likely to impinge on the rights of the accused, why is that?

The guidance for investigators

If the application made for special measures includes video-recorded evidence being presented as the witness' evidence in chief, then that evidence has to be obtained and recorded in accordance with the practice guidance. The guidance to investigators who interview young witness has been developed since the Criminal Justice Act 1991 provided for the facility for video recording of young witness' testimony. Guidance took the form of, 'The Memorandum of Good Practice on Video Recorded Interviews for Child Witnesses for Criminal Proceedings' (Home Office, 1992). This memorandum was amended and developed, and there are several additional editions and reprints. New legislation has followed developing the 'special measures' available for vulnerable witnesses to deliver their evidence in court, and the guidance outlining how interviews should be conducted has developed to keep pace. The current guidance is formalised within 'Achieving Best Evidence in Criminal Proceeding' (Ministry of Justice, 2011). This publication brings to together guidance on approaches and practice when dealing with vulnerable witnesses in general, and includes specific guidance regarding young witnesses. This important guidance addresses how young witnesses should be approached from the initial planning and assessment through the formal evidence gathering process and the court. It outlines how interviews at each stage should be carried out and is directly related to research that addresses issues of reliability and suggestibility outlined previously. The guidance describes which special measures may be applicable in which specific circumstances and how special measures should be applied for and implemented.

The initial investigation stage may well be undertaken by professionals who are not formally trained to interview children; in particular, police officers, social workers or medical staff, among others, are quite likely to come across incidents that involve the victimisation of children that require further investigation. It is also true that the same professionals may have to deal with the initial contact with children who are witnesses to serious criminal cases. It is important that such professionals have a basic understanding of the process involved and of the issue of suggestibility of and influences on the child witness. 'Achieving Best Evidence in Criminal Proceedings' (Ministry of Justice, 2011) outlines the importance of the questioning style adopted at this stage.

> *Where it is necessary to ask questions, they should, as far as possible in the circumstances, be open-ended or specific-closed rather than forced-choice, leading or multiple.*

> *Ask no more questions than are necessary in the circumstances to take immediate action.*

This early questioning is essentially to assess the nature of the incident to be dealt with. Although the early investigation and questioning may uncover evidence, that is not the primary object at this stage. If the child gives a spontaneous full account, that account should not be interrupted, but recorded accurately. The record should include time, date, location and the identity of others present when the account was delivered.(Para 2.6, 'Achieving Best Evidence in Criminal Proceedings', Ministry of Justice, 2011) The information gained at this stage is used to gauge the seriousness and nature of the incident or offence, so that when planning the investigation, due consideration can be given to the level of specialist investigator required and also to special measures being applied for under the Youth Justice and Criminal Evidence Act 1999. If early questioning is carried out precipitously and without due consideration for the law and associated guidelines, the facility of all or some of the special measures may be lost and the value of the young witness' evidence lost to the court. It is also possible that the quality and admissibility of that evidence might be diminished.

REFLECTIVE TASK

Using your knowledge and understanding of the concepts of reliability and credibility, consider how the questioning and investigation might influence a vulnerable young witness. Include in your consideration the long-term impact such inappropriate questioning might have on the rights of the witness and the accused.

Cases involving young victims of abuse come to light through a chain of referral; that chain will often involve an adult/carer who is known to the child but not a child protection professional. This initial 'disclosure' might precipitate strong emotions in that adult. The early interaction between the child and that adult might influence how the child reacts in subsequent investigative interviews.

REFLECTIVE TASK

Consider likely reactions of adults/carers to disclosures of abuse, and the impact they might have on a young vulnerable witness.

The early investigations may be carried out by less specialist practitioners from any of the agencies that are involved in child care and protection. Health, education, social work and police practitioners are all liable to have to conduct these early investigations at some time during and as part of their main duties. Local safeguarding committees arrange multi-agency training so that professionals can understand the correct way to question young witnesses in the early stages of disclosure. This training is important if the quality of the evidence provided by young witnesses is to be enhanced by the special measures available.

Accommodating vulnerable witnesses in the investigative process

During criminal investigations, the police have responsibility for the investigation (Laming, 2003). The police have the experienced resources to carry out criminal investigations which is seen as a key part of the responsibility of the police. Where child witnesses are involved in serious cases, the level of skill required is high and of a very specific specialist nature.

Any investigations involving young witnesses can by their nature be complex and emotive, and this coupled with the issues of competence, reliability and credibility makes the area one where a high level of training and knowledge is required by investigators if the best evidence is to be obtained from young witnesses or victims. While the 'special measures' available provide opportunities to enhance and improve the testimony of the young and vulnerable, they can only do so if properly applied in the correct circumstances. A particular 'special measure' will assist a particular individual in a particular situation; it is, therefore, important that investigators and advocates understand not only what the measure is but how it might assist the witness. The investigators and advocates involved need to appreciate how the measure will assist the young witness or victim and how the particular measure proposed will enhance the ability of the witness or victim to provide the best evidence possible for the benefit of the court. The measures also have to be seen as part of the whole investigative process, and in complex and serious cases, the police will have early consultations with the Crown Prosecution Service to ensure that special measures are appropriately considered.

This chapter has explored the basic concepts of reliability and credibility and briefly outlined how the criminal justice system has developed the law and procedures relating to the use of child witnesses. While each section has been approached separately so that the issues are clearer and can be considered alone, in practice, it is important that you understand how each links and supports the other. The issues that you have considered within this chapter should also be considered alongside those addressed in the chapter within this book on 'Safeguarding Young People'. While not every investigation will lead to criminal proceedings, evidence obtained by the investigation may be utilised by professionals within the safeguarding system. It is through that holistic understanding of the law, procedures and the young witness that the best evidence is achieved and young witnesses are best served by practitioners in the field of criminal investigation and child protection.

FURTHER READING

Bull, R, ed. (2001) *Children and the Law*, Blackwell – This text gathers together research and will help you appreciate the amount of research available and the progress that has been made in this area.

Ministry of Justice (2011) *Achieving Best Evidence in Criminal Proceedings: Guidance on Interviewing Victims and Witnesses, and using Special Measures.* Available online at http://www.justice.gov.uk/guidance/docs/achieving-best-evidence-criminal-proceedings.pdf (accessed 9 June 2011) – This practice guidance is used by practitioners in the field; you should be able to identify how the theory and concepts discussed earlier influence practice and practice development.

REFERENCES

Bruck, M, Ceci, S J and Hembrooke, H (2001) Reliability and Credibility of Children's Reports: From Research to Policy and Practice, in Ray Bull (ed) *Children and the Law*. Malden: Blackwell.

Butler-Sloss (1988) *Report of the Inquiry into Child Abuse in Cleveland 1987*. London: Home Office.

Goodman, G S, Tobey, A E, Batterman-Faunce, J M, Orcutt, H, Thomas S, Shapiro, C and Sachsenmaier T (2001) Face-to-Face Confrontation: Effects of Closed-Circuit Technology on Children's Eyewitness Testimony and Jurors' Decisions, in Ray Bull (ed) *Children and the Law*. Malden: Blackwell.

Home Office (1992). *The Memorandum of Good Practice on Video Recorded Interviews for Child Witnesses for Criminal Proceedings.* London: Home Office.

Ministry of Justice (2011) *Achieving Best Evidence in Criminal Proceedings: Guidance on Interviewing Victims and Witnesses, and Using Special Measures.* http://www.justice.gov.uk/guidance/docs/achieving-best-evidence-criminal-proceedings.pdf (accessed 9 June 2011).

Laming (2003) Recommendation 99 in the Victoria Climbie Inquiry Report. London: Her Majesty's Stationery Office.

Pigot (1989) *Report of the Advisory Group on Video Evidence.* London: Home Office.

cps.gov.uk – www.cps.gov.uk/victims_witnesses/ (site provides guidance on special measures and how witnesses are supported through the criminal justice process).

Her Majesty's Inspectorate of Constabulary – www.hmic.gov.uk/Inspections/JointInspections/Pages/home.aspx (provides access to HMIC inspection reports on victims, witnesses and child protection).

npia.police.uk

Scottish Government – www.scotland.gov.uk/Topics/Justice/law/victims-witnesses/guidance-information/child-witnesses-1 (describes the Scottish approach to young witnesses in the criminal justice system).

G v DPP 2 All ER 755. – *All England Law Reports*. Butterworths/Lexis Nexis

Criminal Justice Act 1991

The Youth Justice and criminal Evidence Act 1999

9 Safeguarding children and young people

CHAPTER OBJECTIVES

By the end of this chapter you should have:

- gained an understanding of the historical context of the current safeguarding arrangements in England and Wales;
- gained an understanding of the current legal frameworks and structures that support safeguarding arrangements in England and Wales;
- understood the role of the police in safeguarding young people, operationally and in the child protection case conference;
- gained an understanding of the role of the police in investigating cases of abuse against young people, as crime investigators and as providers of information for all the child safeguarding agencies;
- gained an understanding of the specific roles and expertise of the agencies involved in safeguarding children;
- appreciated the links between, and interdependency of, agencies whose duties include safeguarding young people and how those links must function;
- appreciated that despite changes in procedures it is how those procedures are implemented that has the major influence on the safety of children and young people.

LINKS TO STANDARDS

This chapter is linked to Skills for Justice, National Occupational Standards Policing and Law Enforcement (2010).

GC11 Respond to allegations or suspicions of child abuse.

Introduction

This chapter reviews the development of child protection and child safeguarding structures; in particular, it outlines the development of and catalysts for the multi-agency approach that now exists. The chapter considers the role of the police as criminal investigators and a safeguarding agency within this structure and how effective communication between agencies best serves the child. The chapter should be considered alongside Chapter 8, 'Young People as Witnesses'.

Children and young people can be the victims of crime like other members of society. This chapter considers the crimes committed against children and young people that fall into the broad definition of 'child abuse'. It looks at how the investigation of those criminal offences has developed and how criminal investigations can provide evidence that is used within the safeguarding procedures. We examine the current arrangements for safeguarding children and young people in the United Kingdom and how the criminal investigation and safeguarding procedures link together in the best interests of children. It includes concepts of information sharing and how child safeguarding case conferences function. This chapter briefly looks at criminal legislation and its development but is primarily concerned with the function of the police and other agencies within the child safeguarding arena.

One of the roles of the police is to enforce the law and to bring offenders to justice. The criminal legislation in the field of child safeguarding includes both specific offences that are only relevant to children and offences that apply to both adults and children in general. The Children and Young Persons Act 1933 is still current and outlines the offence of child cruelty, an offence that is specific to children. Section 1 of the act broadly defines an offence that includes assault, ill-treatment, neglect and abandonment. The police will commonly be involved in investigating the offence of child cruelty as part of their role within the child safeguarding arena.

While the Children and Young Persons Act 1933 includes assault within its definition of child cruelty, there are also other different crimes of assault contrary to the Offences Against the Person Act 1861, and they too are relevant for young people and adults.

Sexual offences have been defined by a number of different acts including those of 1956 and 1985. The Sexual Offences Act 2003 totally repealed the Sex Offenders Act of 1997 and almost all of the Sexual Offences Act 1956 which, until this change, had been the primary legislation for sexual offences. The 2003 act redefined some offences and included new offences, some of which affect young people in particular, such as the raising of the age range for victims of sexual offences from 16 to 18 years – this includes offences involving child pornography. The above is a very brief summary of some of the criminal law that can come into play in child safeguarding, and there is not room to fully explore the criminal legislation in this chapter, and students should research this area elsewhere.

The vulnerability of children and young people is a key concept to understand. Young people are vulnerable in particular ways. Think about how the young have to rely upon others to protect them. Young people do not have the life experience of adults, and judgements they make can be naive. Chapter 8 explored some definitions of vulnerability, which will help you understand the concept in the safeguarding arena. In some circumstances, parents and carers who should be fulfilling the role of protector do not do so and such young people rely on the police and other agencies to ensure their safety. This chapter describes professional roles, policy development and impact, and legislation relevant to roles and policy, and provides the reader with an appreciation of the complex interactions in the child safeguarding arena.

Historical context

It was the investigation of sexual offences, in particular, such as the offences in Cleveland in 1987, outlined below, that highlighted problems with the early arrangements for what was then known as 'child protection'. The private nature of any sexual crime presents investigators with problems, in particular the problem of corroboration, and this may be heightened when the victim is a child. The evidence of children was traditionally treated with scepticism and corroboration was required to prosecute such cases. (The legal issues that impact the evidence of children are examined in more detail in Chapter 8.) That corroboration was often sought in the form of medical evidence, therefore the medical profession and the medical assessment model played a key role.

The cases subject of the 'Inquiry into Child Abuse in Cleveland 1987' (Butler-Sloss, 1988) demonstrated the difficulties encountered in such investigations and highlighted the disjointed approach to child protection at that time. Agencies involved in child protection, and the investigation of sexual abuse in particular, approached the investigation with little co-ordination. The relationship between the agencies in 1987 was not governed by the procedures in place today; the Butler-Sloss report outlined a relationship driven by mistrust and agency agendas. There was little appreciation of how one agency's actions impacted the operation of another. The procedures that were in place had not driven the agencies to work together, and as a result, communication was poor, and actions were motivated by differing agency-led agendas. This lack of co-ordination and trust led to overloading of some agencies but also critically worked to the detriment of the victim. In the Cleveland cases, abuse was diagnosed by medical professionals using one particular symptom and method of examination which in itself was seen as abuse and attracted the title 'double victimisation'. The method of examination was itself invasive and could be seen as abusive. Deer (1988) described the method in *The Sunday Times*.

> After the daughter's disclosure, the children were then on the receiving end of ill-treatment of a different kind. 'Dr Higgs did not introduce herself, nor her

colleagues,' the official solicitor's staff noted from two of the girls. 'She told them to strip – she inserted a stick and cotton wool into their 'privates' and it hurt a little. They were rolled over for their bottoms to be examined and this did not hurt.'

(10 July 1988)

This was the medical process used by Dr Higgs. Because of differing roles and requirements of other agencies, including the police, further medical examinations were carried out. Given the nature of the allegations (sexual abuse, including anal penetration), those further procedures were also invasive and intimate.

Multiple victims were identified leading to multiple arrests, but in the end, there were no criminal convictions. Investigators from both the police and the social services found their actions being determined and driven by the medical team concerned. The lack of consultation and co-ordination meant that diagnosis by clinical staff led to the instigation of a series of reactions from the police and social services. In effect, decisions regarding the welfare of the children, including the removal of children into the care system, were being precipitated by only one piece of the information jigsaw. The medical evidence was given a high priority and not considered alongside information held by social services, the police, education and other agencies. In these cases, Lady Butler-Sloss found that there was mistrust between the agencies and a lack of communication; this led to many of the victims being removed from the family home and into local authority care and during the investigations being medically examined several times, as one agency would not trust the evidence of another's expert.

The cases demonstrate the importance of communication, information sharing, trust and a case management structure within which the victims' interest is paramount. The policy outcome to the report can be said to form the foundation of current 'safeguarding' arrangements. As a direct consequence of the events in Cleveland and the subsequent report by Lady Butler-Sloss in 1988, legislation followed that set new objectives for child protection and recognised and formalised the need for 'multi-agency' cooperation and working methods in the field. The Children Act 1989 (s1) set out for the first time:

That the welfare of the child is paramount.

The associated publication, 'Working Together' (HMSO, 1991), outlined how the key Child Protection Agencies should work together and included the importance of information sharing and joint decision making. The legislation and the 'Working Together' document ensured that new structures were considered and implemented and multi-agency procedures were designed and adopted.

It is useful to appreciate how child protection has developed into safeguarding, and as the legislation is amended and procedures are altered, it important to understand the issues that are shaping the new approaches.

119

R E F L E C T I V E   T A S K

The Butler-Sloss inquiry identified lack of communication and co-ordination as major faults in the investigation of child sexual abuse in Cleveland between 1987 and 1988. What factors might have led to those faults? Consider the impact that multiple examinations have on the child. Why were such multiple procedures taking place? What was the overall impact on child protection in general?

Safeguarding structures

Under the Children Act 1989 Local Authorities were given a general duty to safeguard and promote the welfare of children within their area, who are in need (HMSO, 1991, p 1). Working Together Under the Children Act 1989 (HMSO, 1991) was issued under Section 7 of the Local Authority Social Services Act 1970, and while not of the force of statute, it required compliance from local authorities unless there were exceptional circumstances which might justify variation from the guidance it contained. 'Working Together' directed that Area Child Protection Committees (ACPC) should be formed by those agencies working within the child protection arena, and those agencies should also agree the terms of reference for the ACPC. The guidance also suggested that representatives should be senior officers, or senior professionals, from all the main authorities and agencies in the area which are involved in the prevention and management of child abuse (HMSO, 1991, p 6). Those main authorities and agencies include the police and health, education and the local authorities.

The guidance within 'Working Together' was the first national framework aimed at co-ordinating the responses of child protection agencies. The guidance incorporates and develops the findings of the Butler-Sloss inquiry in order to provide a more comprehensive child protection service.

R E F L E C T I V E   T A S K

The guidance in Working Together specifies 'senior officers'. Why is it important that senior officials are engaged in the safeguarding process? Consider the comments about co-ordination and trust made within the Butler-Sloss report and think how the new ACPC might have achieved co-ordination and trust.

Since the Cleveland cases and the resultant legislation and guidance, there have been other tragic landmark cases, and the resulting inquiries and reports have sought to influence and improve the safeguarding arrangements for young people in England and Wales. These cases offer important learning and understanding of how child safeguarding procedures work, and how procedures are always vulnerable to the way they are implemented by managers and workers in practice.

High-profile cases of child abuse tragically continue to occur and make headlines, and despite 70 public inquiries into child abuse since 1948, the number of children who die as a result of non-accidental injury in the United Kingdom has remained static at around 80 every year for 30 years (Health Committee, 2003).

Among those 70 public enquiries are a number that have had national impact including enquiries following the deaths of Maria Colwell in 1973; Jasmine Beckford and Tyra Henry, both in 1984; Kimberley Carlile in 1986; Leanne White in 1992; Chelsea Brown in 1999; Victoria Climbié in 2000; Peter Connelly (Baby P) in 2007 and Kyra Ishaq in 2008. The deaths of these children all share many points of similarity that have been identified by subsequent enquiries. When considering the report by Lord Laming into the death of Victoria Climbié, the House of Commons Health Committee (2003) quoted Peter Beresford as follows:

> Her death has become one of those major modern occasions where there seems to have been a collective sense of empathy for a stranger's fate. She has become an embodiment of the betrayal, vulnerability and public abandonment of children. The inquiry must mark the end of child protection policy built on a hopeless process of child care tragedy, scandal, inquiry, findings, brief media interest and ad hoc political response. There is now a rare chance to take stock and rebuild
>
> Peter Beresford, Professor of Social Policy, Brunel University

The committee recognised the landmark nature of the case and recognised the repetitive cycle that child protection policy had followed; however, despite this recognition, there have been further tragic deaths that have followed this supposed watershed in child protection.

We will now consider the report of Lord Laming into the death of Victoria Climbié in more detail. Victoria Climbié died in the intensive care unit of St Mary's Hospital, Paddington, on 25 February 2000, aged 8 years and 3 months. Lord Laming was appointed in April 2001 to chair an independent statutory inquiry into the circumstances leading to and surrounding the death of Victoria Climbié, and to make recommendations 'as to how such an event may, as far as possible, be avoided in the future'.

The Report of the Inquiry was published on 28 January 2003 (Laming, 2003), and in it he considered three key questions.

1. In this day and age, in this country, how could this have happened?

2. How could such bad practice go on for so long, undetected and uncorrected?

3. What can we do about it?

In the report, Laming identified that the interventions needed to prevent the tragedy would not have required great skill or made heavy demands on the staff concerned; indeed, he identified that sometimes all that was needed was that a manager did their job. That job included basic actions such as reading the case file and asking pertinent questions of staff. Earlier in this chapter, we have considered the development of multi-agency procedures, following identification of lack of communication and co-ordination by Lady Butler-Sloss (1988) in Cleveland. Lord Laming in this 2003 report expressed his amazement that nobody in the agencies *had the presence of mind to follow what are relatively straightforward procedures on how to respond to a child about whom there is concern of deliberate harm.* Laming revisits these same issues in his 2009 report, 'The Protection of Children in England; A Progress Report', following the death of Peter Connelly (Baby P).

REFLECTIVE TASK

There have been a number of enquiries into child deaths over the years. Research two such cases mentioned above, identify similarities in the management failures of the cases and try to identify why the similarities keep on occurring.

Legislative impact

The Butler-Sloss inquiry of 1989 led to the Children Act 1989 and the associated guidance in Working Together (HMSO, 1991).

Following Laming's 2003 report, legislative changes followed with the enactment of the Children Act 2004. Section 11 of this act places a statutory duty on key professionals and organisations to make arrangements to safeguard and promote the welfare of children; this includes the establishment of Local Safeguarding Children Boards (LSCBs). LSCBs replace the former ACPCs (not Northern Ireland or Scotland) and membership includes the following.

- Local authorities and district councils.
- Police.
- Probation service.
- Youth offending service.
- Health.
- Connexions service (England).
- Children and family courts advisory and support service (Cafcass).
- Local secure training centres (where applicable).
- Prison service (where applicable in that establishments within the LSCB area accommodate young people).

A key issue identified by Laming was the accountability of the managers and leaders of those entrusted with protecting children not being direct enough, and that many managers saw their role as managing an administration and acting at a strategic level. While it is true that good administration is essential to good practice, it is only a means to an end, and administration should not be the outcome by which success is judged. People who occupy senior positions have to be held to account for the service they deliver to the vulnerable young people whom they serve. Do strategy, management and administration secure safety for vulnerable young people?

REFLECTIVE TASK

Research the Children Acts 1989 and 2004. What are the key changes? Do these changes affect the role of police officers working in the safeguarding arena? How has accountability been strengthened? Within England, reference needs to be directed to Every Child Matters; in Wales, Rights to Action and the All Wales Child Protection Procedures; in Northern Ireland, the ACPC, Regional Policy and Procedures and Co-operating to Safeguard Children; and in Scotland, Getting it Right for Every Child.

The role of the police in safeguarding children

Previously in this chapter, you have seen that senior officers of all agencies are required to meet in safeguarding committees; the police are one of these agencies and the police's important role in safeguarding is signalled by this requirement. You will recall that in the safeguarding arena, both criminal and family law legislation are relevant, and police officers taking on this very specialist role need to appreciate the legislation, criminal and family that it used to provide the best outcome for children in need. Lord Laming stated that where there are criminal investigations into child abuse, those investigations are the police's responsibility (Recommendation 99 The Victoria Climbié Inquiry). The National Police Improvement Agency (NPIA) provides guidance for police officers in 'investigating child abuse and safeguarding children' (NPIA, 2009). The following policing priorities are set in NPIA.

- Protect the lives of children and ensure that in the policing of child abuse, the welfare of all children is paramount.

- Investigate all reports of child abuse and neglect and protect the rights of child victims of crime.

- Establish the investigation of child abuse and the safeguarding of children as a mainstream activity.

- Take effective action against offenders so they can be held accountable through the criminal justice system, while safeguarding the welfare of the child.

- Adopt a proactive multi-agency approach to preventing and reducing child abuse and neglect and safeguarding children.

(NPIA, 2009)

Review the above policing priorities and identify how they reflect the recommendations of Butler-Sloss and Lord Laming. Why do the priorities stress safeguarding and welfare, as well as investigation and detection?

Safeguarding children and investigating child abuse and neglect is not just the responsibility of specialist child protection police officers; the nature of policing means that most operational policing personnel will, at some time in the course of their duties, come into contact with children, and so must be aware of the role that they play in safeguarding their welfare. The role of the police in safeguarding children can be divided into a number of separate but interlinked areas.

Quick response incidents that are focused on and driven by child safeguarding concerns

There are incidents the police attend that are entirely focused upon and driven by child safeguarding concerns (e.g. police attend in response to call from concerned neighbour who has noticed infants being left alone unsupervised for long periods). The initial response to such incidents will be by generalist officers in the course of their normal patrol duties. It is important that officers understand and investigate such calls with thoroughness. The subsequent organisational responses will depend on the assessments made at this stage. Officers need to gather wide-ranging information including descriptions of children and adults involved. Such descriptions need to include condition, behaviour and physical characteristics. The environment also needs to be described: issues such as cleanliness, animals, food heating and sanitation are important and need to be noticed, investigated and recorded. It is quite possible for a generalist patrol officer to be the initial resource from any agency at a potentially serious incident, and it is also possible for that officer to successfully intervene, secure support for and prevent harm to the child. In incidents where non-specialist officers respond and identify possible neglect, they have to both investigate and gather evidence, but primarily they have to act in the best interests of the child. Section 46 of the Children Act 1989 empowers police officers to remove children to suitable accommodation if the constable has reasonable cause to believe that otherwise the child would be likely to suffer significant harm. The section also states that the police must, among other things, notify social services, in line with the multi-agency ethos of safeguarding legislation. If the situation is not recognised and the appropriate procedures followed at this stage, children's welfare may be compromised.

Safeguarding concerns that are peripheral to the incident concerned

The police service provides a 24-hour emergency response, as well as less critical and driven contacts. Through the duty of the police to investigate and prevent crime, regular contacts are made with members of the public, often at unguarded moments in peoples' lives. These contacts can often include entry into peoples' homes. It is during these routine and emergency contacts that the police must sometimes consider what may be child safeguarding matters that may not have been the initial reason for contact (e.g. police attend house in response to a call to investigate a burglary and while investigating officers notice suspicious bruises on child). It again might be necessary to utilise s46 of the Children Act 1989. Interventions using the powers of the Children Act are extreme, and officers must always consider the impact on the welfare of the child and ensure that the action is proportionate and the risk of significant harm is real.

In both these general situations, officers must be aware of indicators of possible abuse; as summarised above, more detailed guidance is provided by the NPIA in pages 22–25 of its document, 'Guidance on Investigating Child Abuse and Safeguarding Children' (second edition) (NPIA, 2009)

REFLECTIVE TASK

Consider which legislation gives the police the power to enter property and remove children if need arises. Would the police officer require permission and consent to do this? Using the NPIA guidance, describe what signs a police officer might look for in assessing the likelihood of child abuse being present

---

Complex investigations of safeguarding driven matters. These matters are usually investigated by specialists in child protection from both the police and the social services. Such investigations may involve staff from any agency that has contact with or holds information on the child or its family. These cases, managed through a joint agency approach, differ from the generalist response outlined above in that they involve multi-agency assessments and planning of interventions, ensuring a coordinated and effective approach from all the agencies to what can be long-term case management. These more protracted enquiries can follow emergency interventions as outlined above, as well being precipitated by safeguarding agency concerns about a family.

To recap, we have considered three different catalysts to safeguarding interventions, two types of emergency police intervention and the complex planned intervention. While the emergency interventions are vital, they will always lead to consideration of planned and co-ordinated plans and interventions. The emergency intervention will be a catalyst for considered, co-ordinated multi-agency responses to safeguard the child.

Investigations of criminal child abuse or neglect are the responsibility of the police, and the judgements and decisions regarding prosecution are made by the Crown Prosecution Service in the normal way; those decisions will be informed and influenced by information from all the agencies, as well as the evidential consideration discussed in Chapter 8. Running alongside the criminal investigation will be the safeguarding procedures which will now be discussed in more depth. Students should keep in mind that prosecution is not always the outcome of child abuse enquiries, and in many cases, the investigation leads to other protective safeguarding actions. All the agencies' actions must be driven by concern for the welfare of the child, which is paramount at all times. During investigations, multi-agency strategy decisions will be made, that will include where the child resides and with whom. As well as evidence gathered about a particular occurrence, the safeguarding agencies will consider information about the background and history surrounding the case. This might include criminal records, police intelligence logs, medical history, information from schools and social services records. When considering the information available, agencies judge whether the child is likely to suffer, or is suffering, significant harm. While the concept of significant harm was introduced by the Children Act 1989 and was identified as the threshold that justifies compulsory intervention in family life in the best interests of children, there is no close definition of the concept within the legislation. The NPIA offers the following explanation of significant harm:

> *There are no absolute criteria on which to rely when judging what constitutes significant harm. Consideration of the severity of ill-treatment may include the degree and the extent of physical harm, the duration and frequency of abuse and neglect, the extent of premeditation, and the presence or degree of threat, coercion, sadism and bizarre or unusual elements. Each of these elements has been associated with more severe effects on the child, and/or relatively greater difficulty in helping the child overcome the adverse impact of the maltreatment. Sometimes, a single traumatic event may constitute significant harm, for example, a violent assault, suffocation or poisoning. More often, significant harm is a compilation of significant events, both acute and long-standing, which interrupt, change or damage the child's physical and psychological development. Some children live in family and social circumstances where their health and development are neglected. For them, it is the corrosiveness of long-term emotional, physical or sexual abuse that causes impairment to the extent of constituting significant harm.*
>
> (NPIA, 2009)

REFLECTIVE TASK

Think of examples that might fall into the above classification of significant harm, and identify the evidence that would drive you to reach that conclusion.

Having considered 'significant harm' as a concept, we must now look at different definitions of child abuse and neglect that would constitute that concept.

Definitions of child abuse and neglect

Abuse and neglect are forms of maltreatment of a child. Somebody may abuse or neglect a child by inflicting harm, or by failing to act to prevent harm. Section 53 of the Children Act 2004 amended section 17 and section 47 of the Children Act 1989, so that before determining what, if any, services to provide to a child in need under section 17, or action to take with respect to a child under section 47, the wishes and feelings of the child should be ascertained as far as is reasonable and given due consideration (Jones, 2003).

Child safeguarding procedures identify four categories of abuse and neglect:

1. *Physical abuse* consisting of assaults on the victim that result in injury. It can include striking, shaking, scalding, drowning and other ways of inflicting physical harm on the child.

2. *Emotional abuse*, where the child's emotional needs are neglected and ignored, leading to emotional and mental damage to the victim. Emotional abuse can include conveying to a child that it is worthless or not wanted. While this form of abuse is present in most forms of abuse, it can be the primary form in some cases.

3. *Sexual abuse*, where a child is forced or enticed to take part in sexual activities.

4. *Neglect*, which is defined by s1 Children and Young Person Act 1933 as when *anyone over the age of sixteen years wilfully, assaults, ill-treats, neglects, abandons or exposes child in a manner likely to cause unnecessary suffering or injury to health*.

(Welsh Assembly Government, 2008)

Earlier in this chapter, we considered some of the tragic landmark cases that demonstrate the extreme consequences of failing to implement correct procedures. At this stage, we need to appreciate the aims of the procedures and how they might work when functioning correctly. At all times, the aim is to secure the welfare of the child, and in many cases, the best way of achieving that is not by prosecution or by removing the child from its home environment, but it may be secured better by leaving the child with its natural carers and ensuring support and monitoring takes place. There needs to be a mechanism that considers all the information and intelligence available and then how to go about achieving the best outcome for the child and that mechanism is the 'child protection case conference'.

The child protection case conference

A child protection case conference is a meeting involving the child and all relevant professionals who know, or have information about, the child, their family and their circumstances. The conference provides an opportunity to share information and concerns. Discussions will consider the level of risks to the child and to make plans, which will lead to improvements promoting safeguarding and protection.

It may be recommended that Children's Services Social Work Departments involve the courts to ensure the safety of the child. It is important to note that the initial child protection conference is not a court of law and has no legal powers of its own.

Who may attend the conference?

- Parent(s)/carer(s).

- The child if he or she is old enough.

- The child's teacher or a representative from their school.

- Family doctor.

- Health visitor/school health advisor (with their manager).

- Education welfare officer

- Officer from the area Police Child Protection Unit.

- Local authority's legal adviser.

- Social worker (with their manager).

- Families.

- Minute-taker to make a written record of the meeting.

- Anybody else relevant who is involved with the child.

Police officers present may be helped by the discussion at the conference to decide what if any police action or criminal investigation is needed. It is important to remember that the conference is about the welfare of the child.

The conference will be chaired by an independent reviewing officer. The reviewing officer is usually employed by Children's Services Social Work Department; they are independent of the professionals who have been involved in the assessment and of the people who are present at the conference.

Decisions

The conference will follow an agreed agenda which all those attending will see beforehand. Part of the conference will be to get an understanding of the family and establish what events led to the conference. This will be done by hearing what everyone has to say about events leading up to the conference. The conference will also consider information held about the family and the child that is held by the different agencies present. Following this, the conference will have to consider the following.

- What these facts tell us about any possible risk to the welfare and safety of the child, and how strong that risk is.

- Whether anything needs to be done to protect the child and how quickly this may happen.

- Whether the child needs a child protection plan. The requirements for this will be explained to you and will be available at the conference.

The conference as a whole will discuss what needs to be done to ensure that the child is protected. The views of all who attend the conference are taken into consideration and inform the decision making process.

The child protection conference is a formal meeting that provides the forum for information sharing about a particular child. This information will be sourced from professionals who have had dealings with the child and/or who hold relevant information. The importance of sharing information cannot be over-stressed, and pieces of information held by individual agencies may seem irrelevant when considered in isolation and in the context of the holding agencies' responsibilities; however, when considered as part of an overall picture, they may take on new importance.

The information presented at the conference is used to inform decisions about risk, significant harm and care plans. The information should be presented in the form of a written report from each contributor. In most cases, officers of the police child protection team will fulfil the function of attending case conferences and will present the known information held by the police.

The importance of communication between agencies is identified as crucial. This point has been reinforced by various reports into child fatalities due to abuse, including Lord Laming in his reports following the deaths of Victoria Climbié and Peter Connelly. Consider also the importance of communication within a large compartmentalised organisation such as a police force. The various departments rely upon each other to provide information, and if the welfare of a child is to be protected, then it is vital that information passes both from departments to child protection officers and from child protection officers to other departments. If the flow of information is not free and complete to the child protection officers, that information will not be presented at the case conference and that will hinder the task of safeguarding the child subject of the conference. If the information does not flow from the child protection officers to other departments, other opportunities to protect that child, and possibly others, might also be missed by, for instance, Criminal Investigation Departments and Uniform Patrol officers.

The case conference is not the end product of the safeguarding process; it is a forum that ensures supports and plans are put in place to safeguard the child, and it is, therefore, important that agencies are aware of the decisions made by the case conference in order that relevant agency contact can be put into the context of those plans.

CASE STUDY

Graham is a nine-year-old boy who attends at primary school. His attendance is erratic. When he attends, he is a quiet boy and tends to sit on his own. It is clear that he is not the cleanest of boys, and on occasions, the other children make fun of him because he smells. Graham's mother is recently separated from her partner and has two other children – a girl aged 4 and a boy aged 8 months. There has been no social work involvement in the family, and apart from the services of a midwife and health visitor connected with the birth of the younger boy, the health service has had no recent contact. The police have been called to the home of Graham on two occasions. On both occasions, neighbours called because they could hear shouting and crashing in Graham's home. No arrests have been made. This morning Graham has attended at school and has a fresh bruise on the side of his face, he says 'Mummy did it'.

How would a case conference help to protect Graham?

What information might make the picture clearer and where would it be found?

What do you see as possible interventions that might help Graham?

Child safeguarding is a complex area of policing, and the current arrangements have been influenced by a series of landmark cases: in 1989 Lady Butler-Sloss's inquiry lead to the first legislation and guidance that acknowledged the need for a multi-agency approach to child safeguarding and those procedures have been developed and improved following other tragic cases including Victoria Climbié and Peter Connolly. Despite those improvements, experience indicates more tragedies will occur. Safeguarding is seen as a mainstream policing activity (NPIA, 2009) and needs competent professional police officers who are capable of working with the criminal law as detectives and investigators and with family law to protect children by means other than criminal prosecution. In Butler-Sloss's inquiry into the Cleveland Case in 1987, and Laming's reports following the deaths of Victoria Climbié (2003) and Peter Connolly (2009), the issues of communication and information sharing have been a recurring major failure in the systems for protecting children. Knowing procedures and supporting them with efficient administrative systems will only work if people apply them rigorously and managers manage them with likewise.

FURTHER READING

All Wales Child Protection Procedures, Welsh Assembly Government, 2008. Available online at www.awcpp.org.uk

Getting it Right for Every Child. The Scottish Government, 2008. Available online at: www.scotland.gov.uk/Topics/People/Young-People/childrensservices/girfec

Child protection procedures are prepared by all local authorities and are available online, and should be read to further understand how this multi-agency approach functions.

Guidance on Investigating Child Abuse and Safeguarding Children (second edition). National Police Improvement Agency. Available online at www.npia.police.uk/en/14532.htm – (NPIA, 2009). This publication details the police role and includes specific guidance; it should be read in conjunction with child protection procedures to give you a clear picture of how the two link together.

REFERENCES

Butler-Sloss (1988) *Report of the Inquiry into Child Abuse in Cleveland 1987*. London: Home Office.

Deer, B (1988) Why We Must Now Start Listening to the Children. *The Sunday Times* (London), 10 July.

Health Committee (2003) *The Victoria Climbié Inquiry Report (July 2003). Sixth Report of the House of Commons Health Committee Session. RCGP Summary Paper 2003/09 Committee Session 2002–3. (Ch1).* Available online at www.publications.parliament.uk/pa/cm200203/.../cmhealth/.../570.pdf (accessed 17 May 2011).

HMSO (1991) *Working Together Under the Children Act 1989.*

Jones, D P H (2003). *Communicating with Vulnerable Children: A Guide for Practitioners.* London: Gaskell.

Laming (2003) *Report into the Death of Victoria Climbié*. House of Commons Health Committee.

Laming (2009) *The Protection of Children in England: A Progress Report*. London: Stationery Office.

NPIA (2009) *Guidance on Investigating Child Abuse and Safeguarding Children* (second edition). National Police Improvement Agency. Available online at www.npia.police.uk/en/14532.htm (accessed 17 May 2010).

Welsh Assembly Government (2008) *All Wales Child Protection Procedures*. Available online at www.awcpp.org.uk

USEFUL WEBSITES

http://wales.gov.uk/topics/childrenyoungpeople/publications/rightstoaction/?lang-en (Welsh Assembly Government, 2004b, Children and Young People: Rights to Action).

http://wales.gov.uk/publications/circular/2007/1637402/?lang=en (Welsh Assembly Government, 2004a, Safeguarding Children – Working Together under the Children Act 2004).

www.scotland.gov.uk/Publications/2008/09/22091734/0 (the Scottish Government, 2008, Getting it Right for Every Child).

www.scotland.gov.uk/Topics/People/Young-People/children-families/17834/12076 (the Scottish Government, 2003, Protection of Children (Scotland) Act).

LEGISLATION

Children Act 1989

Children Act 2004

Children and Young Person Act 1933

Offences Against The Person Act 1861

Sexual Offences Act 2003

Index